ROUTLEDGE LIBRARY EDITIONS:
THE GERMAN ECONOMY

Volume 2

REPLACEMENT COSTS AND ACCOUNTING REFORM IN POST-WORLD WAR I GERMANY

REPLACEMENT COSTS AND ACCOUNTING REFORM IN POST-WORLD WAR I GERMANY

GRAEME W. DEAN, FRANK L. CLARKE AND
O. FINLEY GRAVES

Routledge
Taylor & Francis Group

LONDON AND NEW YORK

First published in 1990 by Garland Publishing, Inc.

This edition first published in 2018
by Routledge
2 Park Square, Milton Park, Abingdon, Oxon OX14 4RN

and by Routledge
711 Third Avenue, New York, NY 10017

Routledge is an imprint of the Taylor & Francis Group, an informa business

British Library Cataloguing in Publication Data
A catalogue record for this book is available from the British Library

ISBN: 978-1-138-29360-1 (Set)
ISBN: 978-1-315-18656-6 (Set) (ebk)
ISBN: 978-0-415-78647-8 (Volume 2) (hbk)
ISBN: 978-1-315-22732-0 (Volume 2) (ebk)

Publisher's Note
The publisher has gone to great lengths to ensure the quality of this reprint but
points out that some imperfections in the original copies may be apparent.

Disclaimer
The publisher has made every effort to trace copyright holders and would welcome
correspondence from those they have been unable to trace.

Replacement Costs and Accounting Reform in Post-World War I Germany

Graeme W. Dean, Frank L. Clarke, O. Finley Graves

GARLAND PUBLISHING, INC.
New York / London
1990

Library of Congress Cataloging-in-Publication Data

Dean, G. W.
Replacement costs and accounting reform in post-World War I Germany / Graeme W. Dean,
Frank L. Clarke, O. Finley Graves.
p. cm. — (New works in accounting history)
Anthology of texts, translated from German, accompanied by the 3 authors' commentary.
Includes bibliographical references.
ISBN 0-8153-0006-9 (alk. paper)
1. Replacement of industrial equipment—Germany—Accounting—History. 2. Cost
accounting—Germany—History. I. Clarke, Frank L. II. Graves, Oliver Finley. III. Title. IV.
Series.
HF5681.R34D43 1991
657'.73—dc20
91-3847

Manufactured in the United States of America

Printed on acid-free 250-year-life paper

Acknowledgments

The authors express appreciation to Walter Thanner and Warwick Rodden for provisional translations of Geldmacher [1920] and Mahlberg [1920]. The final revisions are ours and entirely our responsibility. We are grateful for grants from Price Waterhouse (Newcastle) and the Accounting and Finance Foundation of The University of Sydney and for the support of The Universities of Mississippi, Newcastle, and Sydney. The help of Deborah Hichens in typing the manuscript and arranging the presentation of accounts and tables also deserves recognition.

Translators' Note

The texts included in the present anthology have been translated *dem Sinne nach*, that is, according to meaning rather than verbatim. Yet we believe that we have remained faithful to the originals, capturing in particular the correct idiom and the tenor of the works. We have, for example, avoided interpreting ambiguous passages; such passages remain ambiguous in the English. In several instances lengthy German sentences have been simplified either by creating two or more sentences or enclosing explanatory clauses in parentheses. Parentheses, accordingly, are both the authors' and ours, although the material enclosed is entirely original. Footnotes, too, are the authors', although we have changed their format slightly and used italics where the authors used various forms of emphasis. Material in square brackets is ours.

Material in the Preface and Commentary to this anthology draws from and elaborates on the exploratory work in this area by Graves (1985, 1987 and 1989), Clarke and Dean (1986 and 1989), Dean and Clarke (1989) and Graves, Dean and Clarke (1989). Original citations for the items included in this anthology are, in chronological order (the order of their inclusion), as follows:

1. Willi Prion, "Depreciation and Inflation" (Abschreibungen und Geldentwertung), *Plutus*, 15 September 1920, pp. 285-88.

2. Willi Prion, "Replacements and Acquisitions during Inflation" (Ersatzanschaffungen und Neuanlagen unter dem Einfluß der Geldentwertung), *Plutus*, 27 September 1920, pp. 334-37.

3. Walter Mahlberg, "Economic Relativity" (Wirtschaftsrelativität), *Zeitschrift für Handelswissenschaft- und Handelspraxis*, October 1920, pp. 133-36, 182-86 and 195-97.

4. Erwin Geldmacher, "Accounting Problems" (Bilanzsorgen), *Industrie- und Handelszeitung*, October 1920, pp. 364, 378, 385, 392, 398 and 406.

5. Georg von Schlesinger, "Depreciation or Replacement?" (Abschreibung oder Ersatz), *Werkstatttechnik*, 1 October 1920, pp. 506-7.

6. Gustav Kast, "Faulty Cost Accounting" (Falsche Industriekalkulation), *Industrie- und Handelszeitung*, 16 October 1920, p. 1.

7. Theodor Schulz, "Faulty Cost Accounting" (Falsche Industriekalkulation), *Industrie- und Handelszeitung*, 5 November 1920, pp. 1-2.

8. Theodor Schulz, "Faulty Cost Accounting" (Falsche Industriekalkulation), *Industrie- und Handelszeitung*, 6 November 1920, pp. 1-2.

9. Richard Buxbaum, "Depreciation, Replacement and the Value of Money" (Abschreibung, Erneuerung und Geldwert), *Die Bank*, November 1920, pp. 686-96.

10. Richard Buxbaum, "The Effect of Inflation on Cost Accounting" (Der Einfluβ der Geldentwertung auf die Kalkulation), *Industrie- und Handelszeitung*, 1 December 1920, pp. 1-2.

11. Fritz Schmidt, two chapters from "Organic Accounting in the Framework of the Economy" (*Die organische Bilanz im Rahmen der Wirtschaft*) 1st ed., Leipzig, 1921.

> Part C (pp. 59-61, 65-100), "The Organic Balance Sheet."
> Part D (pp. 100-119), "Organic Income Calculation."

CONTENTS

PREFACE

Politico-Economic Background

Contributions to the replacement cost debate contained in this anthology appeared in the immediate post-World War I period of social, economic and political chaos in Germany. Counter revolution from the Right was establishing ascendancy over the socialist revolution of 1918, and German industry was enjoying the benefits of the Weimar government's inflationary fiscal policies. That background was a catalyst for the development of the ideas underlying those contributions to the accounting literature.

Socialist Revolution

In November 1918, immediately prior to the signing of the armistice, socialist revolution spread across Germany. On 4 November workers in Kiel joined the demonstrations of sailors who had refused the German Naval Command's orders to move ships for a final, decisive battle with the British. The rebellion spread first to the various Naval bases across northern Germany and then, as political demands became the impetus for rebellion, to the urban centers of Germany including Hamburg, Hanover, and Cologne. On 7 November Kurt Eisner had called for an uprising among workers in Munich and declared Bavaria a Socialist Republic, and on 9 November, workers left their stations in the factories of Berlin and marched on the city center. In face of these demonstrations, the monarchy collapsed and Kaiser William II fled to Holland.

Throughout the first week of November, Workers' and Soldiers' Councils had sprung up across Germany, and on 10 November the Workers' Councils of Berlin assembled and on behalf of the council movement in general recognized a coalition of Social Democrats and Independent Socialists under the leadership of Friedrich Ebert as the legitimate government of Germany. (The Army, hoping to prevent the country from falling into the hands of radical revolutionaries, had thrown its support behind Ebert on the ninth). Ebert immediately declared a Republic and called for the election of a National Assembly.

Revolution struck industry as well. On 15 November representatives of the trade unions and industry reached the Stinnes-Legien Agreement, according to the terms of which the bargaining rights of unions were recognized. In addition, workers in firms with fifty or more employees gained the right to have an elected committee (a shop council) to oversee, in tandem with management, the implementation of collective bargaining agreements. Employees, further, were to enjoy equal representation with management on arbitration boards. Employers also agreed to re-employ returning soldiers and to introduce the eight-hour working day.

Elections for the new National Assembly took place as scheduled on 19 January 1919, with the Social Democrats, the German Democratic Party, and the Center Party - the three republican parties - winning 76.2% of the votes. It was decided that the seat of the new government would be in Weimar. Berlin was too closely identified with the monarchy and the military.

The Counter Revolution

Despite the apparent popular support for the Weimar Republic in January 1919, a counter revolution from the Right made itself felt as early as the spring of 1919. Already in January the Free Corps, voluntary units of former Army officers financed by industry, were brutally crushing rebellion on the Left: when, immediately prior to the elections of the nineteenth, the Sparticist League (radical communists) occupied the press district of Berlin, including the building housing the official newspaper of the Social Democrats, the Free Corps marched on the area and suppressed the revolt. Indeed, the Free Corps was active throughout the early months of 1919 quelling attempts by the extreme Left to assert the Workers' Council system of governance in various parts of the country, and on 1-2 May the Army itself moved to overthrow the communist government that had seized power in Munich in April.

Consensus support for the Weimar government was dealt an especially hard blow on 7 May when the terms of peace were handed down at Versailles, for it proved much harsher than Germany had anticipated. Germany lost all her colonies, 13% of her territory, and 90% of her merchant fleet. In addition, the Army was to be reduced to a mere 100,000 men. The latter provision, in particular, deeply embittered many Right-wing officers who could no longer anticipate a privileged post-war career. And although the treaty itself was in effect a forced one, the Weimar government suffered blame, and the parties on the Right were able to exploit the resentment among the general population:

> The war, it was argued, had not been started by the Germans, but by the Allies; the war had been lost, not because the Army had been militarily defeated; on the contrary, it was alleged to have been unvanquished on the battlefields. Nor had the country been defeated and driven into the revolutionary upheaval because of the leadership's reckless and inflexible policies; instead the collapse of the home front had allegedly been caused by a minority of left-wing revolutionaries and Jews who, financed by the allies, were supposed to have undermined popular morale. Worse, in November 1918 this minority was said to have seized power by toppling the monarchy and establishing a republic. It had also signed the 'nefarious' Treaty of Versailles . . . (Berghahn, 1982, p. 730).

Anti-Republican sentiment on the part of the Free Corps expressed itself concretely in the Kapp Putsch of March 1920. Free Corps units in Berlin revolted when the government sought to disband them, and the Reichswehr refused orders from Ebert to suppress the revolt. Ebert and his ministers were forced to flee to Stuttgart, and the Free Corps, with the approval of the military, installed a former civil servant, Wolfgang Kapp, whose avowed goal was to dissolve the National Assembly. The Weimar government was only saved by a general workers' strike, which left Kapp and his followers powerless and forced their capitulation within four days. When an army of 50,000 workers in the Ruhr, known as the "Red Army," refused to lay down its arms without a guarantee against further military coups, however, the Reichswehr and Free Corps moved into the area and brutally restored order. The shift to the Right on the part of the middle classes manifested itself three months later in the elections of June 1920 when the anti-Republican, nationalist parties won over 33% of the vote and the Weimar parties lost their majority.

Economic Expansion, Inflation, and the Ascendancy of Industry

Weakened by its loss of popular support (the brutality of the Reichswehr in the Ruhr had also alienated the far Left), the Weimar government pursued a policy of economic expansion to maintain employment levels and stem further social unrest. After the austerity of the war years consumer goods were in much demand; new austerity measures, which might have been appropriate given the war-bond debt the government faced, would only have caused deeper resentment. Thus, the government promoted industrial growth while at the same time rationing basic foodstuffs and maintaining rent controls. And the policy of expansion had yet another advantage: because it fuelled inflation it reduced the financial burden of the war debt and the reparations demands of the Allies.

Industry, in the meantime, profited from the Weimar government's economic policies. As it expanded it invested in new plant and equipment whose current replacement value rose with inflation. It financed its expansion, however, by incurring debt, debt whose value fell with inflation. Indeed, the debt was often effectively worthless when payment fell due.

As to inflation itself, its roots lay in the method the Reich government chose to finance Germany's participation in World War I, that is, the abolition of the gold standard and the rediscounting, on an unlimited basis, of short-term treasury bills to cover its notes. Because of the resultant increase in the floating debt during the war years (from .3 billion marks in July 1914 to 48.2 billion in October 1918), the dollar/mark exchange rate rose from .998 in August 1914 to 1.77 in November 1918, while the wholesale price index rose from 1.09 to 2.34 (Holtfrerich, 1986, p. 17 [1913 = 1]).

The inflationary, expansionist policies of the Weimar government in the immediate post-war years (after dropping by approximately 25% from 1918 to 1919 [Holtfrerich, 1986, pp. 200-01], the index of production in Germany rose from 37 to 54 between 1919 and 1920 and from 54 to 65 between 1920 and 1921 inflated the mark at an even greater rate (*ibid.*, p. 204), [1928 = 100]) . Indeed the dollar/mark exchange rate rose from 1.77 in November 1918 to 9.12 in 1919 and the wholesale price index from 2.34 to 6.78. By November 1920, the exchange rate had risen to 18.39 and the wholesale index to 15.09. In November 1921, the same exchange rate stood at 62.84 and the wholesale index at 34.16 (*ibid*, p. 17). Table 1 reflects the month-by-month movements of the dollar/mark exchange rate (E) and the wholesale price index (W) for the years 1919-21.

Table 1

**Month-by-Month Movement of the Dollar/Mark Exchange
Rate and the Wholesale Price Index, 1919-21**

Month	1919		1920		1921	
	E	W	E	W	E	W
January	1.95	2.62	15.43	12.56	15.46	14.39
February	2.17	2.70	23.60	16.85	14.60	13.76
March	2.48	2.74	19.97	17.09	14.87	13.38
April	3.00	2.86	14.20	15.67	15.13	13.26
May	3.06	2.97	11.07	15.08	14.83	13.08
June	3.34	3.08	9.32	13.82	16.51	13.66
July	3.59	3.39	9.40	13.67	18.26	14.28
August	4.48	4.22	11.37	14.50	20.07	19.17
September	5.73	4.93	13.81	14.98	24.98	20.67
October	6.39	5.62	16.23	14.66	35.76	24.60
November	9.12	6.78	18.39	15.09	62.64	34.16
December	11.14	8.00	17.88	14.40	43.72	34.87

Source: Partial reproduction of Holtfrerich (1986), Table 1, p. 17.

To be sure, the mark stabilized considerably between May 1920 and May 1921 as a result of depression abroad and the advantageous position on the world markets Germany enjoyed as a result of the depreciated mark. (Significant inflation reasserted itself in May 1921 when the Allies made their final reparations demands of 132 billion gold marks, a demand that immediately caused a loss of confidence in the mark). As noted above, however, industry continued to expand throughout the 1920-21 period. As it did so (and as the counter revolution from the Right gained momentum), it began to strengthen its position vis-à-vis the trade unions. As to the attitude of industry towards organized labor during this period, Berghahn (1982, pp. 68-69) observes that

> one must not underestimate the determination of many employers in major branches of Industry to launch offensives against the gains of the working-class movement and to resort to the powerful weapon of lock-outs to change the post-war industrial balance in their favour. The abolition of the eight-hour workday in 1923, one of the major and long-fought-for gains of 1919, and the collapse of the ZAG [Central Cooperative Union] in 1924 provide strong pointers that old hostilities continued to be very deep. Although the methods of the industrial roll-back were different from the ones that were simultaneously deployed in the

political sphere by the anti-Republican Right, the employers' moves must be seen within the broader context of the counter-revolution of the early 1920s.

Price Controls

In Germany economic goods and foodstuffs of all types were the subject of *price maxima* controls - part of the war-time controls (*Zwangwirtschaft*) - from August 1914 onwards.[1] The impact of these price and other administrative controls were still being felt in the immediate post-War period notwithstanding the process of *decontrol* introduced after 1918. For instance, price controls on the products of the iron and steel industry were lifted in 1919, whilst "bread and bread grains were not decontrolled until the end of 1922" (Holtfrerich, 1986, p. 92). Other price controls and their duration are given in Holtfrerich, Table 24, pp. 87-88.

It is worth noting that some financial scribes claimed that these "price and other administrative controls" had suppressed price increases during and immediately after the war because the focus of these initiatives had been to protect "the interest of the urban consumers" in Germany, in contrast to other countries like the U.K. where *minimum* price controls "indicated a policy pursued undeniably in the interests of producers." (Holtfrerich, 1986, p. 85). This had the effect in Germany of distorting efficient product mixes. As Holtfrerich appositely notes, "production shortages [occurred and there was] an adjustment of the product mix in order to escape the effects of price [maxima] regulations and other controls on profitability" (p. 87). Industrial dislocation and pent up pressure for price increases and their justification were inevitable.

Summary

It was in the atmosphere described in these paragraphs that the articles contained in this anthology appeared in the German financial and industrial press. Thus, Georg von Schlesinger defends recognizing additional depreciation on apparently fully depreciated

---

[1]   Holtfrerich (1986, pp. 30-32, 79-94 and 190-91) provides a description of specific price controls implemented during the war and the process of decontrol occurring immediately after the war.

assets vis-à-vis a puzzled shop council member and warns that employees will be out of work if equipment is not maintained and the worn-out plant has to close. Thus, Erwin Geldmacher argues that businesses are "bleeding to death" despite apparent substantial profits and that the matter has locked workers and employers in grim conflict. Witness also Schmidt's relative value principle. The authors, in general, defend depreciation and cost accumulation based on replacement cost as necessary to maintain a company's asset base and, concomitantly, employment levels. Apparent excess profits, they argue, are not profits at all. Indeed, a tax on historical cost income is a tax on capital as is a tax on (replacement cost) depreciation reserves. Balance sheet reform - and tax reform - are urgent indeed if industry is to survive intact. And only replacement cost depreciation and cost accumulation render balance sheets and profit-and-loss accounts correct in the face of inflationary pressures. In short, replacement cost accounting was essential if industry and the German economy were to prosper. These and other issues are further explored in our commentary. It is our hope that this study will aid in the piecing together of the development of replacement cost accounting ideas in Europe and the Anglo-American countries.

References

Berghahn, V.R., *Modern Germany: Society, Economy and Politics in the Twentieth Century*, Cambridge: Cambridge University Press, 1982.

Childs, David, *Germany Since 1918*, New York: St Martin's Press, 1980.

Holborn, Hajo, *A History of Modern Germany, 1840-1945*, New York: Alfred A. Knopf, 1969.

Holtfrerich, Carl-Ludwig, *The German Inflation 1914-1923*, translated by Theo Balderston, Berlin: Walter de Gruyter, 1986.

I. REPLACEMENT COSTS AND GERMAN

ACCOUNTING REFORM:

ABSTRACTS

1. Depreciation and Inflation[1]
Dr. W. Prion

Businessmen recognize depreciation as amounts set aside annually out of sales revenues to cover the replacement or reproduction cost of plant.   Under the conventional model, accumulated annual charges and the scrap value of plant serve to purchase new plant.   But as prices change and as technology improves, those amounts may be insufficient to cover replacement.   Accordingly, the additional cost must be recouped out of future revenues. Inflation exacerbates the problem, for then the depreciation set aside in terms of units of gold-mark book value will not cover the depreciation in terms of their paper-mark equivalents.   One solution is to cease depreciation until the paper-mark depreciated value equals the gold-mark unit value.   The gold-mark balance may then exceed (in terms of its purchasing power) the paper-mark value.   A secret reserve will be created.   A risk in these periods of high taxes is that these reserves may attract tax.   To reduce this possibility one may charge additional depreciation and secrete the amounts away in the liabilities section of the balance sheet.   Though this procedure provides a financial cushion, it distorts the accounting data and is not a good sign financially. Inventories, goods in process, and finished goods are expected to provide content in the balance sheet, but in many balance sheets inventories are recorded especially low, creating further secret reserves.   It would be reasonable to treat the balance in the inventory account in the balance sheet as gold marks.   In the general interest of the economy, depreciation reserves due to inflation should not be taxed.   The ultimate amount of the depreciation reserves attributable to inflation cannot be determined precisely.   If the depreciation were not affected by the losses from any subsequent downward trend on prices, additional tax would become a possibility.   It is most unfortunate that today the tax authorities only allow a small, totally inadequate, increase in depreciation because of inflation.

---

[1]   *Plutus*, 15 September 1920, pp. 285-88.

2. Replacements and Acquisitions During Inflation[2]
Dr. W. Prion

Inflation has necessitated increased charges for depreciation to meet increased costs of replacement. Whereas some companies have created secret reserves of the kind outlined in the previous article, many have chosen to charge replacements against current revenues of the year of replacement and to leave the asset account at its pre-war balance. Current and subsequent years' profits are distorted as the plant benefits the production of many years. A major factor encouraging that practice has been the fear that prices may decline in the future and excessive depreciation charges may become taxable. There also has been the desire to avoid raising additional share capital to finance replacements, to the extent that the depreciation fund fell short and the attendant prospect of having to pay out higher dividends arose. Charging plant acquisition costs in the current year's profit and loss has artificially kept subsequent years' costs down and inflated subsequent years' profits. Conversely current profits are artificially deflated by the immediate expensing of catch-up maintenance and replacement charges in that year. Businessmen have assumed that during inflation, high depreciation charges are uncertain, jeopardize the profitability of the enterprise and are financially imprudent, unless the increased charges are incorporated into the current year's costs of production - thereby escalating the selling prices of goods. This practice becomes financially prudent for the enterprise, though not necessarily in the best interests of the shareholders as it decreases dividend payouts. By advocating such prudence businessmen have overlooked the likelihood that although a decline in revenues may occur, expenditures would decline too. In pursuing this course of action businessmen have promoted the well-being of their enterprises over economy-wide considerations. Government price control boards may become a necessity to prevent a transformation of caution on the part of businessmen into a major price escalation.

---

[2]   *Plutus*, 27 September 1920, pp. 334-37.

3. Economic Relativity[3]

Walter Mahlberg

Germany is left with a much smaller net worth of assets, yet the primary objective for all Germans is the maintenance of the German economic system. Since 1914 Germany has been unproductive as those who are now well established economically were engaged in unproductive expenditures on, for example, munitions. Values for the average German citizen have not been maintained. And now France treats these unproductive expenditures as profits and demands reparation payments. Paradoxically, the current inflation increases with the decrease in the capacity of the economy to pay the reparations. There is rampant profiteering as inflation spirits away property from its owners. Yet, it is not possible to drop below a certain level of physical property. As it is, physical asset values represent peace-time prices and embody undisclosed (secret) reserves which accrue to shareholders. In contrast, bondholders certainly hold only claims to marks of a diminishing value. Of course, capital may be maintained by the removal [replacement] of assets, and there are strong grounds for arguing that sales prices ought to be raised to facilitate the acquisition [replacement] of physical assets, such as machinery, at current prices. Depreciation quotas or similar accounting procedures are no longer adequate to replace assets. In reality, property capital is decreased when calculations are not made on the basis of future values. Banks which deal with borrowed funds suffer the least from this decrease by virtue of profitable turnover. Meanwhile inflation confiscates private sector capital and converts it into public capital. The weekly journal of the German Social Democrats, *Die neue Zeit,* describes this activity as the Undersecretary for State Julius Hirsch's reprisal plan to nullify the "capital strike" which has resulted from the "reluctance to invest." This arises from the economically intolerable thought of profiteering. All this exacerbates, and to a large extent feeds, the reparations problem, for the peace treaty specifies that Germany pay the highest taxes. German goods effectively have to cross the border and remain out of Germany for repayment purposes. Our output is insufficient to sustain the German standard of living and replenish the gaps in the German stocks of

---

[3]   *Zeitschrift für Handelswissenschaft- und Handelspraxis*, October 1920 pp. 133-36, 182-86 and 195-97.

physical assets. Germany has to practice "social economics" in a "polished style." All this is manifested in the adverse exchange rate which reveals Germany's financial relationship with the rest of the world. For reparations have the same impact as the excessive importation of goods. Accordingly, the exchange rate will be under continuous pressure. In order to replace our stock and pay the compensation demanded, Germany has to bear the brunt of inflation by increasing domestic productivity.   Increased work, restrictions upon all daily needs (along with price control), foreign credits at usurious rates, and swamping by foreign capital, are Germany's future. Neither Communism nor Socialism can relieve that burden - they can only worsen it!

4. Accounting Problems[4]
Erwin Geldmacher

People cannot see that inflation is bleeding businesses to death. Substantial profits were made from the War, but the reported reserves are deceptive. The commercial profit-and-loss account has been sabotaged - even the banks, the business giants, have turned into dwarves. Business calculations are wrong, for they should not be based on the out-of-date acquisition costs, but on the replacement costs valid at the time of sale. Likewise in the setting of prices. This is the only policy which can eliminate the fatal danger in the growing currency depreciation. Mathematically, in times of rapid price rises and inflation, the traditional commercial profit and loss is inapplicable. It entails mathematical nonsense. Expenditures are measured in Reichsmarks of a different character from those of the operating or performance items. Expenditures often occur ahead of time. Some are incurred even in gold-mark terms. On the transactions side there are only the paper-mark figures - each newer amount expressed in buying power taking second place to its predecessor. Thus in the subtraction which ensues two sizes of a different criterion are accounted for in the one difference. As we cannot subtract nordic kroner from German-Austrian kroner, so should we subtract higher value marks from lower value marks? Corruption is turning to plague proportions. Price determination on the basis of replacement prices and wage increases thereon are denounced as profiteering, the withholding of funds from taxation is increasing, and there is deliberate falsification of the balance sheet too. Goods are becoming stores of value in lieu of money as people exploit the economy. Business management is incorrect. Profit calculation is not a matter for businessmen alone. Legislation must be introduced to ensure the maintenance of the "productive bases" of German companies. Balance sheets must be kept interpretable to show this. One way is to legislate to shield from taxation the paper increases in the worth of companies' "initial capital." It is protection, not a cure. For all who can see through the haze of the money sphinx, the view must be that when the monetary system has been renovated, the consuls must not have slaughtered all the economy's "milking cows."

---

[4] *Industrie- und Handelszeitung*, October 1920, p. 1.

5. Depreciation and Replacement[5]
G. Schlesinger

The incorrect understanding of depreciation as an optional charge by accountants has led to confusion as to why tens of thousands of depreciation are being charged with respect to assets already written off in the accounts. Additional, excess depreciation accrues to the enterprise, infusing it with new blood for the replacement of assets. Depreciation is a means of setting aside savings so that plant may be replaced continuously. Many accountants have not taken heed of the depreciation of the currency. Many factory accountants have not noticed the frictionless transition from a gold to a paper currency. When the time comes for replacement, depreciation based on gold-mark balances is insufficient. They use the bookkeeping system as a scapegoat for their own foolishness. Even the sharpest tool wreaks havoc in the hands of the unskilled. However, the tax authorities have not yet recognized the concept of "replacement depreciation," and managers are tempted to undervalue assets, including inventory, rather than create large (though correct) depreciation charges in the accounts. Instead they create reserves to replace assets, thereby distorting the balance sheet which discloses everything but the actual state of affairs. The sad fact today is that the currency is a rubbery unit of measurement. It expands and contracts daily and interferes with the costing process.

---

[5]   *Werkstattstechnik*, Vol. 14 1 October 1920, pp. 506-507.

6. Faulty Cost Accounting[6]
Gustav Kast

Inflation after the war tossed out the principle that one cannot add apples and oranges. For that is what is happening in balance sheets; pre-war gold-mark balances are added to weaker post-war paper-mark balances. As long as cost accounting is viewed as merely a mathematical process the economic changes arising from the depreciation of the mark will be ignored. This is so in respect of depreciation, the purpose of which is to provide sufficient funds to acquire replacement machinery. Industry, unaware that sufficient funds for replacement are not being provided, unknowingly donates hundreds of millions to consumers every day. In comparison the Reich emergency tax is only a trifle. Restating asset values in terms of paper marks and crediting the difference to an "Asset Value Correction Account" would avoid accumulated depreciation on a replacement basis appearing greater than related asset values. Without these steps industry faces catastrophe, as companies actually experiencing losses are paying huge dividends out of capital.

---

[6] *Industrie- und Handelszeitung*, 16 October, 1920, p.1.

7. Faulty Cost Accounting[7]
Dr. Theodor Schulz

Whereas one can agree with the thrust of Mr. Gustav Kast's analysis of the effects of inflation on cost accounting, some of his comments should be challenged.   The value of money sank perpetually, though gradually, even before the war, and the undercharging of depreciation (which he explained) was a phenomenon too.   Every prudent businessman will have provided generous amounts to cover the cost of future replacements, the cost of which would be uncertain.   The problem has only had extraordinary significance since the war.   Even as Herr Kast explains it, the depreciation problem can have a different color. Increasing the depreciation charge as the decline in the purchasing power of the paper mark becomes apparent may still be insufficient to offset the depreciation deficiency up to that time.   Stability of the paper mark in the future is a prerequisite for accuracy of the calculations.   If the paper mark weakens and prices continue to rise, the depreciation included in costs will have to be increased continually.   If the German economy begins to recover, then too much depreciation may have been charged.   This would be the lesser of two evils.   Foreign exchange rates and the prices of goods, in relation to their pre-war levels, provide uncertain reference points for the value of the paper mark.   Even the price of gold has not shown absolute stability.   Prices for plant assets have been variable too. How are the relatively small increases in real estate and farm land to be compared with the extraordinarily big increases in the price of machinery?   Herr Kast's solution is feasible only after the paper mark has stabilized.   Plant and equipment must continue to be valued in gold marks, or on a basis which will be permanent until the economy recovers.

---

[7]   *Industrie- und Handelszeitung,* 5 November, 1920, p. 1-2.

8. Faulty Cost Accounting[8]

Theodore Schulz

Even during periods of stable prices the price of gold did not remain fixed. It also is unlikely, when the present crisis subsides, that the price of gold will return to its pre-war level. We cannot expect prices to be stable in the future. If we were to assume a permanent increase in prices we could adjust balance sheets permanently by scaling up the pre-war paper-mark values by the likely average price increase, say, 250% of the pre-war price. That amount could be recorded in the asset account and any amount by which the actual price exceeded or fell short of the scaled-up value could be placed in another balancing account and expensed as quickly as possible. Accordingly, in each fiscal year the appropriate amounts would be charged against sales and the excess cost credited to the special balancing account. If prices are not stable the Reich tax laws need to be changed to avoid the eventual ruin of a large portion of German enterprises by taxing what really are correct increased paper-mark charges against sales revenues. Of course, the laws must ensure that profits and true secret reserves over normal depreciation do not escape taxation. We must also avoid further negotiations which permit inaccurate conclusions regarding Germany's national wealth and the country's productivity and solvency because our balance sheets reflect extraordinary paper-mark increases of plant assets. Valuing assets net of excess cost would also provide a more reliable basis for determining the market value of stock as well as an entity's credit-worthiness. Such a reliable basis is lacking today. We must be careful not to expropriate large segments of the German economy through the distribution as profits what are not "profits" at all. We should consider statutory action to forbid paper-mark values in the plant and other asset accounts rather than fix maximum percentages of pre-war values as noted earlier, and make the Paper-Mark Excess Cost Account subject to increased depreciation. In such an event, depreciation originally recorded on gold-mark values would have to be increased. It would be rewarding for leading industrial organizations to muster all their means to bring about a change in the tax law. The ideal procedure - from a private sector point of

---

[8]   *Industrie- und Handelszeitung*, 6 November 1920, pp. 1-2.

view - would be to recognize sufficient depreciation to create the means necessary to replace the asset upon the exhaustion of its useful life. These matters are in the interest of the national recovery.

9. Depreciation, Replacement, and the Value of Money[9]
Richard Buxbaum

The immediate concern regarding depreciation and expenditures for replacement is that businessmen have lacked the means to replace assets because of the sizeable inflation. Depreciation eliminates asset balances as the assets become worthless. Indeed, the Commercial Code requires items intended for re-sale to be booked directly with any decline in value; receivables are to be stated at net realizable values. Depreciation thereby accounts for the reduction in the value of assets and is independent of the financing of replacement items. With items not intended for resale it is customary not to write off the reduction in value to the asset concerned, but to record the diminution in a contra account. Propositions by Rathenau, Kast, Prion and Schlesinger that treat depreciation and reserve funds for replacement somewhat as synonyms are erroneous; depreciation and reserves are simply different things. The former relates to facilities on hand; the latter, to future facilities. Both the spirit and juridical interpretations of the law approve the creation of reserves to meet future expenditures. Of course, sober-minded shareholders will demand reserves be limited to amounts in accord with that spirit. The effect on pricing must also be borne in mind. It is advisable to account with care and strictly in keeping with fact, legal requirements, and sound business practice.

---

[9] *Die Bank*, November 1920, pp. 686-696.

10. The Effect of Inflation on Cost Accounting[10]
Richard Buxbaum

Neither the proposal by Kast nor the proposal by Schultz, is practicable. First, the idea that the gold mark and the paper mark differ, that they cannot be summed, is only an aesthetic shortcoming.   Movements in the values of the assets and liabilities stemming from previous years tend to counterbalance. No standard of value for the mark exists, so indexation would serve no lasting purpose. It would only increase the value of plant by the normal rate of inflation, thereby violating the basic rules of mathematics. Likewise, restatement of paper marks as a multiple of the gold mark is quite arbitrary. The matter clears up if one correctly understands the function of depreciation - to eliminate valueless debit positions, to reflect declines in the value of property. Funding replacements is to be effected through legally created reserves for that purpose under §262 of the Commercial Code. Such reserves benefit private enterprise. Price increases lie in the present, even though their impact will take effect in the future when new plant assets are purchased. We must work to gain recognition from the tax authorities for the creation of such reserves. But both depreciation and allocation to reserves ought to be a deliberate, not mechanical, action and too sharp an increase in sales prices avoided. Cost accountants will better be able to function if they understand these principles.

---

[10]   *Industrie- und Handelszeitung*, No. 273, 1 December 1920, pp. 1-2.

11.   C. The Organic Balance Sheet[11]

Fritz Schmidt

The problem is to find a method of accounting that brings to light the changes in value that eddy about the *floating* enterprise. The point of departure for all values is market price, the market determines the values of all goods, both consumer and capital.   In this context the relevant value is current replacement value or reproduction value - the highest price the most marginal enterprise can pay and still earn (1) a normal return on capital and (2) entrepreneurial compensation. In respect of tangible assets the objective is to obtain a combined current value for enterprise assets and liabilities. This objective is achieved by aggregating the current replacement values of the individual items.   The result is the "value of the enterprise." In the context of inflation, it is necessary to distinguish between "real" assets and "monetary" assets. The latter are affected by inflation. This contradicts keeping the value of money nominally constant in today's accounting.   Gains on liabilities are generally offset by losses on receivables. It must be noted, however, that during inflation a larger volume of goods must be sold to repay debt.   Changes in asset values are capital, not income. In organic accounting, therefore, changes in replacement value or reproduction cost are credited to a capital adjustment account, which is adjunct to the capital account itself. This is in marked contrast to conventional accounting according to which changes in values have appeared as gains or losses in the profit-and-loss account. Whilst that procedure may be tolerable when prices are stable, it has a grotesque effect today.   Today's balance sheets are a terrible mess; businessmen and bookkeepers can hardly make sense of them.   Neither can stockholders and other interested parties who have this mishmash of values served up to them. How clear a balance sheet would seem in comparison in which each asset appeared at its current value.   Businessmen need current values to manage!   It is to be noted that depreciation at replacement value harmonizes with the market. Higher revenues give the appearance of higher profits, but actually contain higher depreciation quotas. During periods of stable prices accounting

---

[11]   Two chapters from Fritz Schmidt, *Die organische Bilanz im Rahmen der Wirtschaft* ("Organic Accounting in the Framework of the Economy"), specifically, Part C (pp. 59-61, 65-100), "The Organic Balance Sheet", and Part D (pp. 100-119), "Organic Income Calculation."

according to the dictates of §261 of the Commercial Code gives the same results as accounting according to organic principles. A new school of accounting theorists thinks along business economics lines and tends to recognize depreciation not on historical cost, but replacement cost. Of course in the case of long-lived assets, replacement cost may lie far in the future. Schmalenbach considered future replacement cost as the basis for depreciation, but rejected it since at the time the shortcomings of historical cost were less problematical than trying to determine replacement cost in advance. Prion explained methods which entailed a shift from historical cost to replacement cost near the end of the asset's life, but he balked at the high prices that would result. Mahlberg, in his gold-mark balance sheet, captured the spirit of organic accounting, but he, too, concentrated on replacement cost at point of replacement. Likewise the German Machinery Manufacturers. All these methods distort profits year by year. *Future* replacement value is the wrong standard of measure. Historical cost and future replacement value lie below and above current replacement value respectively. The correctness of using current replacement value is proved by the manner in which its use enables the enterprise to maintain its relative position in the economy. There is no need to consider future replacement value to be sure of having sufficient funds to replace at point of replacement; for the funds after receipt in the form sales revenue will simply appear in a different form in the balance sheet, that is, as an investment in assets that hold their value until time for replacement. Accounting for nonmonetary current assets is much the same. For under organic principles, they, contrary to the lower-of-cost-or-market rule under historical cost, will be valued at replacement value as at the date of sale, the turnover date. Again, differences in value are to be accumulated in a capital adjustment account, as part of the capital of the enterprise. (It should be noted, however, that values for costing and the balance sheet may differ if the *operating* and the *balance sheet cycles* do not coincide). Under organic accounting, equity capital bears all the risks of increases and decreases in values. Thus, under conditions of changing prices, equity capital bears the brunt of the price-level change, whilst debt capital remains unchanged. One has to achieve an "equality of values" in the balance sheet if the relative position of the enterprise in the economy as a whole is to be maintained. Capital must be structured so that price-level changes have the best possible effect - during periods of inflation large amounts of debt capital will enhance prospects of increasing wealth, while if trends reverse conversion into relatively more equity capital must ensue. Overall, the primary task of businessmen is to ensure that the value of every real asset rises or falls at least at the average rate at which prices are changing. At least a normal rate of return indicates that enterprise assets are being preserved.

D. Organic Income Calculation

Income is the surplus after recovery of the cost to maintain enterprise productive capacity relative to the economy as a whole. Indeed, maintenance of relative productive capacity lies at the heart of the replacement cost principle in organic accounting. Such maintenance is achieved by carefully balancing the two spheres of economic activity - the turnover sphere and the monetary sphere.

The principle of cost accumulation and sale at actual cost places all price changes in the monetary sphere; for if all costs required to maintain relative production are not contained in the sales price, additional capital must be raised, whether debt or equity. This situation can lead to enterprise impoverishment during periods of inflation and enrichment during periods of deflation. Costing (and pricing) on the basis of the cost on the day the factor input is consumed can improve the situation. Changes in value that occur between acquisition and production are thereby placed in the turnover sphere. Increases in the prices of factor inputs after cost date must then be covered by raising additional capital.

The boundary between the monetary and turnover spheres shifts according to the date to which we relate cost. If we use actual replacement cost all cash balances and monetary receivables become part of the turnover sphere; if income levels rise sales revenue must be sufficient to include the surcharges necessary to cover full replacement cost on the actual date of replacement, as compared to replacement cost on the date of sale. As the domain of equity capital, the turnover sphere assimilates all increases and decreases in value. Thus, while equity capital increases and decreases with price-level changes, debt capital remains rigidly fixed. Overindebtedness can be avoided only by transforming debt capital into equity capital.

The risk of overindebtedness encourages proportional structuring of the turnover and monetary spheres by relating the replacement cost principle to the cost to replace on the day of sale, that is, when the finished goods change hands in the market. We may usefully call this day "the day of market transfer" or "the turnover date." If costs are based on the replacement cost as of the day of sale, wage earners pay a price containing a cost-of-wages component at the same level as their own current one. A proportional structuring of the national income at the macro level thereby also becomes possible.

Recognition of the difference between the turnover and the monetary spheres at the enterprise level also finds support at the national level, for values in the turnover sphere are real values and thus constitute national wealth. In contrast, values in the monetary sphere are monetary values that arise from the circulation of the national wealth. From an organic point of view the proper value for costing is replacement cost, that is, current cost plus incidental costs to acquire as of the date of market transfer.

Turnover is the precondition of completing the production cycle via sale. But if the cycle is incomplete and inventory is still on hand it will be entered in the organic balance sheet at year-end replacement cost which is not the same as replacement cost for costing purposes. Attempting to use the latter value (being a future value at the balance sheet date) for unsold inventories would mean taking into account increases and decreases in value that arise after the balance sheet date.

The simplest solution is to accumulate historical costs in the inventory account and to revalue them as of the balance sheet date, charging the difference to the capital adjustment account. Thus, under organic accounting, balance sheet replacement cost is not the same as replacement cost for costing and pricing purposes, by virtue of timing.

II. REPLACEMENT COSTS AND GERMAN

ACCOUNTING REFORM:

COMMENTARY

II. Replacement Costs and German Accounting Reform: Commentary

Replacement Costs and Pricing

Conventional cost-accounting mechanisms and the data therefrom are the subject of current inquiry and criticism. Many observers, such as Johnson and Kaplan (1987) and Cooper and Kaplan (1987), contend that cost-accounting data are "too aggregated, too untimely and too distorted" to be relevant to the decision needs of managers. The apparent catalyst for this focus was the relatively poor performances of Western manufacturing firms in the early 1980s when compared to, for example, the performance of Japanese and Korean firms. Similar cries of discontent were heard in 1920s Germany regarding the cost-accounting data produced from what were perceived to be *outdated* or inappropriate for the functions they were to serve. The titles of articles in this volume give an indication of the disquiet: "Faulty cost accounting," "The effect of inflation on cost accounting" and "Depreciation and inflation." The types of solutions proposed in those articles, however, were at variance with those proposed in the modern literature. The current remedies are quite properly described as "old wine in new bottles!" Activity based costing (ABC) is the generic title given to many of the current remedies. ABC involves, in today's idiom, the identification of overhead *cost drivers* and the identification of cause and effect relationships. It is claimed that in today's more automated manufacturing processes that in many instances direct labor should be replaced as the allocation base. Other non-volume related variables, such as the number of transactions or the number of productions set-ups, we are told, are more likely to generate, and therefore be, a better allocation basis.

The product of revising allocation bases is still an accumulation of historical costs as a proxy for a product's value. As such, it could be argued that today's cost-accounting solutions are being sought within the existing historical cost paradigm. Not so according to the proposed remedies of 1920s German business economics movement.

Depreciation and Funds for Replacement

Cost-tracing, costs-attach and cost-plus pricing

Unusual circumstances are conducive to unusual practices. There can be no doubt that the circumstances of post-World War I inflation were socially and economically atypical. There can be equal certainty that the pervading focus in the German accounting literature following the war was to design methods of accounting which would convince the fiscal and regulatory authorities of the ineffectiveness of conventional accounting practices. Particularly so for the assessment and evaluation of the financial position of German industry and commerce.   We might reasonably suspect that the objective of having financial statements disclose an accurate measurement of periodic income and financial position was set aside, if having them do so would not have highlighted the incapacity of the Germany economy to fund the rest of the war reparations and bolster the German campaign to keep those payments to what the Germans perceived to be acceptable proportions. In the 1990s vernacular, those actions would have been targeted as examples of the *economic consequences* motivation driving accounting policy.   It highlights how pliable basic accounting techniques nourished pragmatism in accounting policy choice.

Several matters arising from that pragmatism pervade current accounting: that *costs attach* and are price-traced to products frequently remains as an integral part of determining the basis for sellers' cost-plus-pricing policies; accounting to calculate periodic income and to determine financial position continues to be influential in the development of tax rules and policy; and the idea that depreciation being charged against revenues creates a *replacement fund* which can be drawn upon to fund future replacements of plant and equipment continues to be a theme underlying proposals to incorporate price changes in accounts.

Imbedded in this 1920s German accounting literature are the seeds of the arguments presented in the English-language accounting literature (albeit in a more developed manner) fifty years later and onwards in favor of replacement-price-based depreciation calculations.   Particularly significant is the way in which hints of defects in the replacement-price depreciation mechanism in the German literature went either unnoticed or unheeded when they later were drawn upon to support current costs and replacement price systems in the 1970s and 1980s. Explicit political motivations which drove the German campaign were repeated in the later resurrection of the argument, though clothed then, primarily in a mantle of evolutionary theoretical development.

There can be no doubt that in inflationary times depreciation calculations based on historical cost data understate the numerical value of the appropriate charge in terms of its current general-purchasing-power equivalence. And there can be no reasonable disputation of the proposition that such an historical-cost-based depreciation charge is mismatched against the purchasing-power value of sales and other revenues expressed in terms of contemporary currency units. Those issues alone, however, are insufficient by themselves for drawing the conclusion that current replacement price is the appropriate base for depreciation and cost-of-sales calculations. Though mechanisms that connect cost calculations firmly to an overall framework of accounting for revenues and expenses might bend the argument in that direction.

Two such linkages are imbedded in the German literature this anthology comprises: first, that costs must be traced to products and processes to provide the appropriate contemporary pricing basis; and second, that prices are set by sellers rather than by the prevailing market. That costs attach and therefore must be traced to individual products and services runs strongly through this German literature. Schulz [7] alludes to the need to take the *increased depreciation* into account "in calculating cost and setting prices" and should be "charged to cost of goods sold." Schmidt's concept of a "turnover sphere" draws upon a "cost to date" which traces to products' "changes in value that occur between acquisition and production"; he refers to "cost components," noting "sales revenue representing cost recovery." *Depreciation* is identified as one such attaching cost which, by virtue of its calculation base, is unlikely to be correctly matched in Schmidt's "turnover sphere" to produce either a *correct* inventory *valuation* or a *correct matching* of costs with revenues in contemporary terms for profit determination.

Geldmacher [4] illustrates the contemporary 1920s understanding of the inventory and mismatching problems. "Buying, selling and cost increases tend not to go in fits and starts as they do here." Alluding to the perceived nexus between costs and prices he notes Schmalenbach's observation that if "production costs are to serve price formation purposes

[they] must be based on costs actually paid," thereby explaining the difference between the pre-war pricing mechanism and that currently in force.   Of *necessity*, Geldmacher continues

> the price actually obtained did not result from the costing practices of individual enterprises, but from free-market, often global competition. Price formation was flexibly anchored between supply and demand, and a clinging money gown showed things as they really were.

Geldmacher further revealed the idiosyncratic nature of this brand of cost-tracing and the presumed need of a cost-plus pricing mechanism: "Nowadays anarchy reigns in the economy . . . demand, voracious as it is, must surely grow immeasurably.   And prices along with it."   The German inflation was thus recognized to be a departure from the normal state of affairs.   And the post-war period was deemed to be a time condemned to deviations from the usual acquiescence to the market setting the pace with prices, lest (as Geldmacher explains) the profit-and-loss account became "mathematically nonsensical" by adding and subtracting data indicative of Reichsmarks with different purchasing powers. Buxbaum [9] took things a lot further, noting that " . . . for costing purposes . . . increased reserve allocations are a factor in seeking higher sales prices and greater profit figures." Not that the distortions were perceived to fall evenly across all sectors of the German economy.   True to the received theory of movements in price structures, Geldmacher pointed to   primary production suffering less than German manufacturing industry (as confirmed by Holtfrerich, 1986).   That was an issue which was to be repeated in post-World War II Britain in particular.   We will address that episode below.

The "cost-plus" pricing debate in Germany followed lines of thought similar to those followed in the Anglo-American literature during the late 19th century.   Wells (1978) has captured the essence of that debate.   After citing what is described as a "unique passage in the literature of the period" from Marshall's *The Economics of Industry* (1881, p. 75), Wells rejects the necessary link between costs and prices, noting

> . . . that these calculations [underlying pricing decisions] are *ex ante*, as they must be if a decision is to rest on them; they do not make price dependent on

costs; and they place emphasis on total rather than unit costs and profits. (1978, p. 112)

Earlier in his monograph on *Accounting for Common Costs*, Wells was critical of textbook writers as well as other writers on cost-accounting issues who have adhered to the labor theory of value and the associated notion that *costs attach* to products:

[T]here is no demonstration of the obvious need for the association of overhead costs to products. . . A single figure purporting to be a product cost but which in fact represents this agglomeration of outflows [e.g., current outlays, past outlays and future outlays] is more likely to be dysfunctional than helpful to managers aiming to ensure [via its pricing mechanism] that the firm survives. (1978, pp. 9-10)

Finally on this matter it is apt to recount the observation of the neo-classical economist, Smart (1910):

However great the cost expended on an article, if the public will not have it, all the cost in Christendom will not give it value. (p. 72)

Taxation lobby

(a)   Mismatching and "mathematical nonsense"

A constant theme in the translated literature presented here is the perceived connection between external accounting data and the impetus they might give during inflation for deliberate fiscal action by tax authorities. Particular sensitivity appears to prevail regarding the fiscal authorities' capacity to skim off nominal (illusory) profits arising from the mismatching of (relatively) inflated revenues with historical-cost expenses, including depreciation. Prion [1] draws attention to the need of the tax authorities to recognize "on a timely basis" that *at least* ". . . depreciation . . . increased in proportion to inflation . . . should be tax exempt." Similar themes are pursued by, for example, Kast [6] in his explanation that the restrictions placed on depreciation allowed for tax purposes under the Commercial Code "unknowingly [donate] *millions* to consumers every day . . . . The so

adamantly opposed Reich emergency tax is only a trifle compared to such huge losses "
[emphasis added]. Whilst disagreeing with Kast's call for the Reich Tax Code to be
changed to allow the booking of assets in terms of their current paper-mark equivalents,
Schulz's view on the situation was sympathetic with the general proposition that the
capital base of German industry was being eroded through the tax system. Generally, the
basis for setting prices ignored the excess depreciation of the paper marks in which
revenues were automatically expressed.

Not unexpectedly, substitutes for paper-mark data were sought to present a more
realistic position. Surrogation for gold-mark values through scaling up asset prices to a
predicted pre-war/post-war price ratio of (say) 250% featured in Schulz's [8] solution.
The balance over the actual cost was to be transferred into a paper-mark balancing
account. The remainder was to be charged off to expense immediately, or if it was
considerable, over a twelve-month period and thereby conflict with the Reich Tax Code
regarding depreciation. If the tax authorities did not accede, Schulz explained, a *double
account system* could be used to book the cost of the asset in the conventional plant
account, place the assumed 250% increase in asset value in a Paper-Mark Excess Account
and amortize it at a greater rate under the approval of special arrangements with the tax
authorities.

The novelty and significance of Schulz's suggestion is gleaned from its similarity
with the adjustment technique which appeared subsequently in Schmalenbach's seminal
1921 indexation article (see Graves, Dean and Clarke, 1989).

Particularly worth noting in these contributions to the depreciation debate is that the
idea of a mismatching of costs and revenues focused on the incremental depreciation
charges attributed to the period under review, rather than on the incremental costs
supposedly attaching to related revenues. That is, whereas the *costs-attach* idea appears to
have infiltrated the argument when the focus was on cost accumulation and on its implied
nexus with pricing policy, the idea of costs attaching had a far less significant role when
matching was the focus. In the German political and economic climate of the 1920s it
appears that instead of logic driving the depreciation argument, it had become the servant
of it.

In contrast with Schulz, Geldmacher's explication of the distortions created through inventory price movements in the calculation of cost of goods sold, is more consistent with the *costs-attach* version of the case for taxation relief:

> [M]any a businessman will sit and sweat behind his profit-and-loss figures. It will dawn on him that behind these inflated profit figures are the liquidation results, measured in paper marks, of his *old* stock of operational assets. (*Emphasis added*, [Part III])

But more significant for the general future of accounting thought were Geldmacher's comments on the "mathematical nonsense" of the application of arithmetical procedures to monetary units representative of different purchasing power dimensions. Similar sentiments appear in Kast [5] and von Schlesinger [6]. In the English-language accounting literature this notion became entrenched much later through Sweeney's "mathematically unsound" complaint against "ordinary accounting" in his *Stabilized Accounting* (1936). But Geldmacher [4] had already explained:

> . . . this mathematical nonsense is what is happening in the profit-and-loss account today. Expense items are measured in Reichsmarks of a different character than those of revenue items. The expense side always shows mark amounts of a higher real value than those shown on the revenue side. This is true because all expenses precede revenues and in the interval the Reichsmark loses additional purchasing power. On the expense side there are even gold-mark amounts from pre-war days, namely the annual depreciation quotas that began before the war. [4, Part IV]

The *Reichsmark* could, Geldmacher continued, be compared to a

> folding rule which becomes shorter and shorter, but which in various stages of collapse continues to be used as a . . . 1 m rule, so that a silk ribbon measuring 1 m . . . would be measured as 2, 5, 9 then 12 m successively. It would be mathematical nonsense if one added or subtracted the meter amounts at the various stages.

In a perverse sense that offense of *mathematical impropriety* (Clarke, 1982, p.81) is mismatching of a variety more damaging to the financial integrity of accounting data, than is the "period" type to which the others referred. For whether costs are deemed to attach and whether period symmetry is achieved is of little import if the resulting data are processed in a manner contravening the rules of basic mathematical operations.   That variety of mismatching was the pivotal theme underscoring Sweeney's case for *Stabilized Accounting* and for most of the arguments presented from the early 1950s onwards in support of scaling up conventional accounting data with index numbers.   Significantly, it was raised in this early German literature primarily in the context of a case for injecting replacement prices or reproduction costs into accounts as a major departure from the conventional wisdom.   In contrast, Sweeney's mechanism was essentially a scaling-up of the conventional historical cost data, even though he preferred to have the scaled data approximate replacement or reproduction costs.   Inexplicably, the later push by the Anglo-American professional accountancy bodies for replacement (or current) cost valuations in the 1970s and 1980s made virtually no mention of the need that accounts comply with the canon of *mathematical propriety* (Clarke, p.419).

(b)   Depreciation as a source of replacement funds

That charging revenues for the depreciation of long-lived assets creates a cash reserve to fund the future replacement of assets pervades the German literature in this anthology. Prion [1] was in no doubt that depreciation is based upon "the simple idea of setting aside a sufficient amount of annual sales to cover the replacement or reproduction cost of plant." Von Schlesinger [5] noted the function of charging depreciation is to ". . . set aside savings in such amounts that all plant and equipment . . . may be continuously maintained or replaced . . ."   Kast observed, "Specifically. . . [depreciation's] purpose is to provide sufficient funds to acquire replacement machinery . . ."; an idea with which Schulz concurred, contributing the view that depreciation is not intended merely to recover the historical cost of the assets (which would have been consistent with the simple matching concept), but rather to accumulate "the amount necessary to replace" them.

But that view of the nature and function of depreciation charges along with the belief in the necessity for the charges to be based upon a replacement or reproduction cost basis did not pass unquestioned in the *Betriebswirtschaftslehre*.   In this collection dissent is evidenced in Buxbaum's [9] analysis of the "meaning of depreciation," in his discussion of the problem of providing for replacement of plant and equipment, and in his explanation of the "immediate cause" of the "renewed preoccupation" with those issues.

Buxbaum's commentary is very perceptive. For it contains many answers to propositions appearing in the accounting literature in the 1970s and beyond. First is his observation that "depreciation is the accounting expression of reductions in the values of assets." Here he has recourse to the etymological source, for although he does not state it, the source is *de pretium* - decrease in price. Second is the distinction he draws between depreciation provisions and the creation of a fund for asset replacement. "Depreciation does not have a thing to do with this reserve fund," he notes. Third is his reinforcement of the previous proposition in stating that replacement is to be effected by the creation of reserves *specifically for that purpose*. For the concept of depreciation, he contends ". . . pertains to assets on hand . . . never serves to fund new or replacement items . . . neither can one contend that depreciation in any way serves to 'accumulate' funds." That comment comes very close to suggesting that replacement funding is a problem of either capital raising or cash budgeting. Finally there is his telling comment when drawing upon the example of the Krupp corporation being freed of its obligation to manufacture war munitions, that is, that creating a fund for replacement conflicts with the adaptive nature of business enterprise. *Replacement* is but one of many options available to adaptive enterprises.

In many respects Buxbaum's commentary appears a less politically motivated analysis than those to which he refers - Prion, Schlesinger, and Kast (from this anthology) - each of whom appears comfortable with the depreciation/replacement fund nexus.

Incomplete expositions

Pragmatism appears to have hindered the development of a sound theoretical argument in these German contributions. Clearly, Germany faced several competing and pressing needs exacerbated by the increasing inflation, the funding of the war reparations payments and the crippled state of the post-war German productive capital stock. It is far from clear whether the German authors, whose ideas are the subject of this inquiry, fully understood how their proposed accounting mechanisms to capture asset depreciation were to operate.

In particular it seems that no general answers were forthcoming to what now is labeled the problem of depreciation "backlog."

Prion, for example, notes that the creation of a fund for replacement has to contend with both potential increases in the prices of replacement assets and changes in the purchasing power of money. He thus alludes to the differential impact of inflation on specific prices, their compensatory effect on the aggregative structure of specific price changes and the concept of movements in the general level of prices. But he stops short of actually explaining the mechanism by which the funds "reserved" to absorb the increases in replacement prices are to be accumulated and turned into cash if and when the time for replacement arrives. To the contrary, Prion appears to avoid the difficult question of how *ex post* adjustments to depreciation charges and the reserving thereof can work to create the replacement fund if previously calculated profits have been distributed as dividends or expropriated through the tax system. Whereas the scaling of gold-mark accounts could be effected without difficulty, as also can the creation of the *Paper-Mark Excess Cost Account* proposed by Schulz and Kast's *Asset Value Correction Account*, Prion noticeably declares that "[t]he retroactive effect of this procedure on enterprise profit will not be pursued . . ."

Perhaps the key to the manner in which funds are accumulated, which seems to elude Prion, Schulz and Kast, comes in Schmidt's [11] exposition on the "Organic Balance Sheet." Worth noting is his allusion to the process of *continuous reinvestment* of the depreciation charge:

> [O]rganic depreciation . . . provides enough means to actually acquire a new machine [at an inflated price] when the old one is retired. This seems impossible since total accumulated depreciation is only 6,400M., and 10,000 M. are required. The correctness of the idea becomes clear when one recalls that depreciation is very much at one with the organism of the enterprise and continually adapts to the economy along with it. . . . [D]epreciation at the end of the first year, calculated on the basis of a price level that has doubled, would not be set aside in cash (that would mean removing assets from circulation). Rather, the amount . . . would immediately appear in a different form on the assets side of the balance sheet since it would be used to acquire new fixed assets . . . It would be simplest to assume . . . that the new fixed assets were immediately purchased . . . changes in the values of fixed assets do not necessarily move parallel . . . it is up to the businessman to acquire assets that hold their value.

Clearly what Schmidt has in mind is that if a continuous reinvestment in assets of the kind to which the depreciation charge relates is not feasible, then the investment *as part of the business organism* will increase in value as prices rise and thus make up the difference between the amounts charged against revenues for depreciation and the eventual replacement price faced when the asset in question is retired.

Schmidt's example of reserving only 6,400 M. to meet the current plant replacement cost of 10,000 M. illustrates the continuous investment line of thinking. There, Schmidt appears to mock disbelievers as he explains how, *in organic accounting,* the funds released through depreciation charges are invested in other assets and become part of the organism of the firm and accumulate along with it.

Note, too, Schmidt's allusion to the idea that an immediate investment of the depreciation charge in new fixed assets would *be the simplest to assume.*   That observation, though not pursued by Schmidt any further (for its obvious impossibility in any reasonably complex asset structure), has surfaced elsewhere to support the continuous replacement theme after World War II: for example, Norris (1949, pp.122-124), Brown (1952, pp.100-101), and Edwards (1954, pp.172-176, and 1961, pp.172-176).

Britain's Sandilands Committee presented a case of immediate continuous investment to explain how current cost depreciation would achieve the maintenance of a firm's productive capacity (para. 480). Schmidt's lesser proposition that the depreciation charges be invested in other assets has been a popular approach over the past seventy years too. Compare, for example, Paton (1922, pp.433-439), Mathews and Grant (1958, p. 12), Edwards and Bell (1961, p.193), Gynther (1975, p.123), and the Richardson Report (1976, para. 17.07). Clearly, that notion of continuous reinvestment has retained its appeal for the supporters of the replacement price case. The similarity between modern versions of it and Schmidt's organic concept is most marked. But contrary to Schmidt's framework the modern versions have been presented exclusively in the context of maintaining the firm's productive capacity *per se,* irrespective of what happened to the economy's capital as a whole.

Schmidt's framework suggests interesting implications for the working of an industrial economy. It appears that a number of necessary conditions appear to be satisfied if Schmidt's confidence in the accumulation of the 10,000 M. is to be met. First, the price of the plant for replacement needs to change (increase) in line with the growth rate of the firm. Second, the firm's wealth needs to change in proportion to the change in the overall wealth in the national economy as a whole, if the *relative maintenance of the capital* of Schmidt's firm is to be achieved. And third, it appears that for each of those to occur either every firm in the economy has to pursue the maintenance of its relative capital position in the economy, or differential growth rates for all the other firms in the economy have to accidentally mesh to permit Schmidt's firm to achieve its relative maintenance objective by chance, rather than by design.

It is interesting that Mey (1966) when discussing Limperg and Schmidt alludes to the unlikelihood that Schmidt's relative maintenance objective could be sustained. In particular, contrasting Schmidt's maintenance objective with Limperg's less idealistic variety, Mey points out that firms are *free* to pursue the maximization of their wealth without regard for the objectives of other firms, and certainly without collusion on that score.

It is of contemporary significance that Schmidt's analysis and argument contained the same gaps as existed fifty years later when the continuous reinvestment proposals resurfaced in support of the replacement fund idea.   No explanation arises as to how funds from the reinvestment can be accumulated so as to equal exactly the replacement price in the future.   Generally, during the 1970s debate on such matters it was conceded that it was an impossibility, with the consequence that the claims made for current cost-accounting that profit could be distributed in full and productive capacity remain intact could not be satisfied.   Productive capacity was almost certainly going to be either under- or overmaintained and of consequence income understated or overstated (Clarke, 1982; Dean and Wells 1979).   An additional dimension to the problem in Schmidt's framework is that under his organic accounting the mechanism not only had to maintain a variety of productive capacity, but maintain its relativity with the national productive capacity.   That would involve achieving some variety of harmony with the relative shifts in productive capacity of all other enterprises in the economy, a seemingly impossible mission!   It was certainly a novel twist to the debate.

Schmidt's explanation of organic accounting does not present any clearer understanding of the supposed inevitability of the accounting income/tax nexus than emerged in the inflation and taxation debates following World War II. It has never been explained why tax authorities, for fiscal purposes, ought to be influenced by how accountants calculate income and assess financial position. Supposed linkages are more intuitive than real. It appears reasonable to link capacity to pay income tax with reports of profitable business activity, and it is reasonable to expect the fiscal authorities to monitor what corporations perceive to be increments in wealth to determine who has that capacity (Simons, 1938). But the theory of public finance and the history of income tax law indicate that the derivation of tax rules is as much the outcome of trade-offs between capacity to pay and ease of collection criteria, as it is between idiosyncratic assessments of issues of equity of burden and worthiness of benefit. The only permanent link appears really to be in the use of a common nomenclature in the fields of taxation and accounting. Neither the tax lobby in the U.S. to achieve the tax acceptance of LIFO inventory valuation through its use for accounting purposes during the 1930s, nor the clothing of the push in post-World War II U.K. for replacement-priced-based depreciation and cost-of-goods-sold calculations as *accounting reform* have worked. In both instances the revenue authorities gave concessions of those kinds only when eventually it suited them for fiscal (and or political) reasons unconnected to either the calculation of accounting income or the stating of financial position. Compulsory use of LIFO for accounting purposes, if it is used for tax in the U.S., and the implied restrictions placed upon the use of the stock valuation adjustments variously given during the 1970s and early 1980s in the U.K. and Australia appear no more than token penalties for the concessions being taken up (Clarke, 1982, pp.219-228, and 277-279).

Post-World War II - déjà vu with a difference

There is considerable similarity between the motivations for, and the supporting arguments in favor of, injecting replacement cost or reproduction cost depreciation and inventory calculations into accounting in the post-World War I German accounting literature and the post-World War II U.K. and U.S. literatures. That similarity also applies to countries which generally follow the British or North American accounting traditions, i.e., Australia, Canada and New Zealand. In many respects it has been a case of déjà vu.

Particularly interesting is the parallel between the movement for taxation relief by British industry following World War II and that evidenced in the literature included in this anthology. Although not in anything like the same proportions as experienced in Germany in the 1920s, the post-World War II British economy was under inflationary pressures as the transition to peacetime brought heavy demand for consumer and tertiary goods. Similar also to the previous German experience, British manufacturing industry was severely run down by its conversion to wartime production. Most of the British plant and equipment had been acquired prior to 1940 and the little replacement which had been undertaken during the war was incompatible with peacetime production. Importantly, a considerable portion of British plant and equipment was completely written off for taxation purposes. British industry pleaded the case that tax rates were so oppressive as to be threatening industrial recovery. The pleadings of British industrialists were identical to those which are described in the 1920s German literature, especially those reproduced in this anthology. High taxation rates and the lack of concessions to compensate for rising prices of industrial raw material were the problem. Further depreciation allowances for the plant already fully depreciated under British tax law were not permitted. And depreciation allowances on the remainder being based on pre-war historical costs were much lower than proportionate charges based upon current replacement prices.

Similar to the experience in post-World War I Germany, a considerable amount of the argument claimed that calculating depreciation and cost of goods sold on the basis of current replacement or reproduction cost was also *good accounting* for external reporting purposes. Britain's Millard Tucker Committee commenced its inquiry into the computation of trading profits for taxation purposes in 1949 and was followed by a Royal Commission into the issue in 1951. Neither inquiries found that tax relief of the kind proposed was justified. Curiously they found in favor of a system of *initial allowances* (accelerated depreciation) and generally encouraged companies to reserve funds for replacement as part of their budgetary procedures. Curious and unpopular support for this was given by the Institute of Chartered Accountants in England and Wales in their Recommendation No. XII (1949) and No. XV (1952), to the effect that "profit appropriations" should be made to provide for any shortfall. Arguments presented to those official inquiries had a familiar ring. Britain's Federation of British Industries in response to the Millard Tucker Committee submitted that

> [s]ome temporary adjustment to our taxation rules is essential if the physical capital of industry is not to be seriously depleted. . . the simplest method of dealing with the problem . . . is for additional allowances to be given for taxation purposes (*Report*, 1951, paras. 24,25)

Those sentiments and support for the depreciation replacement fund idea also appeared in the technical literature of the time, for example in Lacey's *The Accountancy of Changing Prices* (1952) and the Research Committee of the Cost and Works Accountants' *Profit Measurement and Price Changes* (1952). But in the same vein as Buxbaum in 1920, the depreciation/replacement fund nexus was disowned, in particular by Norris (1949), Prest (1950) and Wiles (1951).

Similar conflicting arguments arose for the next thirty years in the English-speaking countries (Clarke, 1982, Whittington 1983, and Tweedie and Whittington 1984). Most significant in these arguments are advocations that the depreciation fund notion provides theoretical support for a mechanism to finance asset replacement, and the failure of those promoting the method to satisfactorily answer the depreciation back-log problem (Dean and Wells, 1979).

In the British and North American tradition the push for injecting replacement price depreciation into accounts for *external reporting* purposes appears to have arisen in what has been labeled the "1920s appreciation debate" (Clarke, 1982). Arguments arising in the context of using "fair values" for setting the rate base for utility pricing purposes drifted into the context of external reporting by ordinary industrial and commercial companies. The contextual shift was significant, for whereas the utilities were generally nonadaptable enterprises with respect to their capacity to change the nature of their operations, the ordinary companies into whose affairs the notion of fair value was being transported were infinitely adaptable, able to change their sphere of operations as they chose within bounds of their individual financial constraints. Replacement of current productive capacity was a virtual certainty, *ceteris paribus*, with the utilities; not so, with the adaptive companies. The "fair value drift" was from nonadaptive to the adaptive company setting (Clarke, 1982).

In contrast, the setting in Germany in the 1920s was the opposite. The case for current-replacement-price depreciation was being presented explicitly in the context of adaptable companies - albeit subject to price and other administrative controls. That it was and may have been inappropriate appears to underlie Buxbaum's observation of the potential inconsistency between providing for replacement through the depreciation fund mechanism and replacement not being required (as he aptly explained with respect to the post-war operations of Krupp). Noticeably, no mention was made of anything resembling the U.S. utilities context.

Any fair value drift from the 1920s debate in Germany would have to have been in the opposite direction to that of the U.S. experience. In Germany the drift would have been from the *adaptive* company to the *nonadaptive* company context. It has been déjà vu, with an important difference!

Summary

In 1920s Germany, times were indeed unusual. Industrial equipment was physically exhausted and obsolete, primarily due to the unremitting war effort. The effects of wartime price and other administrative controls were still evident and there was an ever increasing taxation burden associated with the taxation of paper profits (*Scheingewinne*) and the need of the German authorities to meet war reparations. Unusual times also are the catalyst for *novel solutions*. Events in post-World War I Germany were no exception.

Pre-World War I accounting in Germany is best summarized as being balance sheet oriented, having a static focus coupled with the view that only a *monist* approach was valid. Also there was compliance with the conservatism doctrine, specifically the lower-of-cost-and-market rule and the realization principle. Accordingly no *systematic* attempt was made to incorporate adjustments for either price or price-level changes. Of course there were exceptions. Ciompa (1910), Fäs (1913) and Kovero (1912) argued for the supplanting of historical cost data by market-price data - specifically replacement prices by the latter two and selling prices by the former. The monist, essentially static approaches however had their critics, noticeably Schmidt.

Turbulent price movements of this post-World War I period upset this position. The tables from Holtfrerich (Table 1, 1986) and Bresciani-Turroni (Tables 3-5, 1937) captured the fact that the price movements were chaotic and disruptive of trade. This chaos ushered in the revolutionary new paradigm of replacement price proposals evident in the writings translated here, *dualistic* proposals that placed equal emphasis on income determination *and* asset valuation. The most well-developed theory, obviously, is Schmidt's. In the other works contained in this monograph, however, the major elements that re-emerged in all of the subsequent replacement cost proposals occurring in the post-1920s decades of the twentieth century can be found.

References:

Bresciani-Turroni, C., *The Economics of Inflation*, Allen and Unwin, 1931.

Brown, E.C., "Depreciation Adjustments for Price Changes," in the *Effects of Taxation Series*, Harvard University Press, 1952.

Ciompa, P., *Grundriß einer Ökonometrie und die auf der Nationalökonomie aufgebaute natürliche Theorie der Buchhaltung - Ein auf Grund neuer ökonometrischer Gleichungen erbrachter Beweis, daß alle heutigen Bilanzen falsch dargesellt werden*, C.E. Pöschel, Leinberg 1910.

Clarke, F.L., *The Tangled Web of Price Variation Accounting*, Garland Publishing Inc., 1982.

Cooper, R. and Kaplan, R. S., "How Cost Accounting Systematically Distorts Product Costs," in Bruns, W. J. (Eds), *Accounting and Management Field Study Perspectives*, HBS Press, 1987.

Dean, G.W., and Wells, M.C., *Current Cost Accounting: Identifying the Issues*, USARC and ICRA, 1979.

Edwards, E.O., "Depreciation Policy Under Changing Price Levels," *The Accounting Review*, April 1954.

Edwards, E.O. and Bell, P.W., *The Theory and Measurement of Business Income*, The University of California Press, 1961.

Fäs, E., *Die Berücksichtigung der Wertverminderung des stehenden Kapitals in den Jahresbilanzen der Erwerbswirtschaften*, Tübingen 1913.

Graves, O.F., Dean, G.W. and Clarke, F.L., *Schmalenbach's Dynamic Accounting and Price-Level Adjustments*, Garland Publishing Inc., 1989.

Gynther, R., *Accounting for Price Level Changes: Theory and Procedures*, Pergamon Press, 1966.

Holtfrerich, C-L., *The German Inflation*, Walter de Gruyter, 1986.

Institute of Chartered Accountants in England and Wales, Recommendation XII, "Rising price levels in relation to accounts," January 1949.

_____, Recommendation XV, "Accounting in relation to changes in the purchasing power of money," May 1952.

Institute Cost and Works Accountants, *The Accountancy of Changing Price Levels*, Gee and Co., 1952.

Johnson, H.T. and Kaplan, R. S., *Relevance Lost: The Rise and Fall of Management Accounting*, HBS Press, 1987.

Kovero, I., *Die Bewertung der Vermögensgegenstände in den Jahresbilanzen der privaten Unternehmungen mit besonderer Berücksichtigung der nicht realisierten Verluste und Gewinne*, Berlin 1912, Helsinki 1911.

Lacey, K., *Profit Measurement and Price Changes*, Pitman, 1952.

Marshall, A. and Marshall, M. P., *The Economics of Industry*, Macmillan and Co., 1881.

Mathews, R.L. and Grant, J. McB., *Inflation and Company Finance*, Law Book Company, 1958.

Mey, A., "Theodore Limperg and His Theory of Costs and Values," *ABACUS*, September, 1966.

Millard Tucker (Chairman), *Report of the Committee on Taxation of Trading Profits*, HMSO Cmnd. 8189, 1951.

Norris, H., "Depreciation Allocations in Relation to Financial Capital, Real Capital and Productive Capacity," *Accounting Research*, July 1949.

Paton, W., *Accounting Theory, with Special Reference to the Corporate Enterprise*, 1922, (Reprinted) Accounting Studies Press, 1962.

Prest, A.R., "Replacement Cost Depreciation," *Accounting Research*, July, 1950.

Richardson, I.L.M. (Chairman), *Report of the Committee of Inquiry into Inflation Accounting*, Government Printer, New Zealand, 1976.

Sandilands, F.E.P. (Chairman) *Report of the Inflation Accounting Committee*, HMSO Cmnd. 6225, September 1975.

Simons, H.C., *Personal Income Taxation*, The University of Chicago Press, 1938.

Smart, W., *An Introduction to the Theory of Value on the Lines of Menger, Wieser and Böhm Bawerk*, Macmillan & Co., 1910.

Sweeney, H.W., *Stabilized Accounting*, 1936, (Reprinted) Holt, Rinehart and Winston, 1964.

Tweedie, D., and Whittington, G., *The Debate on Inflation Accounting*, Cambridge University Press, 1984.

Wells, M.C., *Accounting for Common Cost*, Center for International Education and Research in Accounting, Illinois, 1978.

Wiles, P., "Corporate Taxation Based on Replacement Cost," *Accounting Research*, January, 1951.

Whittington, G., *Inflation Accounting: An Introduction to the Debate*, Cambridge University Press, 1983.

III. REPLACEMENT COSTS AND GERMAN

ACCOUNTING REFORM:

TRANSLATIONS

1. Depreciation and Inflation[*]

Dr. W. Prion
Professor at the University of Cologne

Depreciation, which the businessman recognizes annually on long-term plant and equipment, is based on the simple idea of setting aside a sufficient amount of annual sales revenue to cover replacement or reproduction cost of plant assets when they are retired. If liquidation of an enterprise is anticipated, the monetary capital invested in productive assets (whose productive capacity is now exhausted) must have been earned or won back from sales. The textbook example is well known: the historical cost of a machine is 10,000 M.; its useful life, 10 years; its salvage value, 1,000 M. Depreciation in this case amounts to 900 M. annually for ten years. At the end of the tenth year - disregarding the effect of compound interest -

1.	salvage value	=	1,000 M.
2.	cash: 10 x 900 M.	=	9,000 M.
			10,000 M.

will be on hand.

But since enterprise continuity is the general rule, the 10,000 M. must serve to purchase a new machine of the same kind and quality and the same economic significance as the worn-out machine. The great stability of prices before the war, along with the tendency for prices to fall as a result of mass production, did much to reinforce the idea that accumulated depreciation represented a plant replacement fund. Of course technical innovation or increased efficiency may lead the manager to purchase a more expensive - and better - machine in place of the old, retired machine. But in this case, as a matter of principle, the additional cost of the new machine would have to be recovered from sales of the goods produced by the new machine, that is, the additional cost will at first have to be funded from capital. Increasing annual depreciation on the old machine to cover the cost of the new machine did not correspond to the understanding of depreciation at the time.

---

[*]   *Plutus*, 15th September 1920, pp. 285-288.

In other words, depreciation was not based on replacement cost, which could only be estimated in any event. The cost of the old machine was to be recovered from the revenues generated by the old machine. The goods produced by the new machine, accordingly, had to bear the cost of depreciation for the new - more expensive - machine. If caution and prudence on the part of the businessman often led him to depart from this principle and actually depreciate more or less on the basis of replacement cost, all the less reason to object since this procedure benefited the financial security of the enterprise. Besides, the practice generally found a natural limit in peace-time prices which fluctuated only rarely.

Inflation twisted this principle in two directions:

1. Plant assets purchased before the war and in the early war years often remain on the books at their old values, that is, in gold marks. Is depreciation even necessary in these cases? Apparently not according to the theory of "value depreciation"; for in terms of today's paper marks such plant assets are worth many times their book values. One could discontinue depreciation on these assets until, through the process of wear and tear, their book values coincided with their current or market values expressed in paper marks. In many cases, however, such coincidence would not be attained since the salvage value of plant assets in terms of paper marks is often still greater than their book value expressed in terms of gold marks. Future paper-mark proceeds in these cases would be greater than values reflected in the books. Accounting gains would result even though depreciation had been discontinued. If one views matters in this way as a matter of principle continuing to depreciate plant assets increases the difference between the assets' gold-mark book values and their values in terms of paper marks or the actual proceeds from their eventual disposal.

But viewing matters in this way fails to take into account that these residual values, even if they are numerically higher than their current book values, are only paper-mark representations that do not cover replacement. For replacement cost in paper marks is ten to twenty times greater the original cost, that is, it may be 40 to 50 times its current book value or future residual value. It follows that depreciation that has been recognized on the gold-mark value of plant assets no longer has the same meaning or purchasing power. It, too, has taken on the characteristics of paper marks - in an arithmetical sense at least - and can regain its former purchasing power only by means of additional allocations from reserves, profits, or capital. The following example will illustrate.

If a machine that was purchased before the war for one million marks and has a book value of 700,000 marks at the end of 1918 and costs 20 million marks to replace at the outset of 1920, an annual depreciation rate of 50,000 marks would not suffice to accumulate the 20 million marks in 20 years. Nor are the 300,000 marks accumulated over the 6 years 1914-20 more than 300,000 *paper* marks, that is, not even ⅓ of the one million paper marks necessary each year to cover the 20 million mark replacement cost. It follows that in recognizing depreciation on plant assets whose book values are expressed in gold marks a multiple of the amount previously charged - a multiple corresponding to the rate of inflation - should be booked. The matter would be clear and simple if the old values were restated in terms of paper marks and depreciation were recognized on the paper-mark values. It would then be perfectly clear that depreciation had been increased merely because of inflation and must be increased if the enterprise is to accumulate sufficient funds for plant replacement and thus enterprise continuity. Restatement of plant assets in terms of paper marks is neither customary nor feasible at present, yet managers are aware of the paper-money character of depreciation and tend to act accordingly. It is not surprising therefore, that depreciation has seemed especially high recently.[1]

Above all, however, one should expect timely recognition of the internal change in depreciation on the part of the tax authorities. Namely, to the extent that depreciation has increased in proportion to inflation - an increase that under certain circumstances can be considerable -, [the income offset] should be tax-exempt, just as any genuine depreciation charge reduces taxable income. Of course in particular cases the extent to which increases in depreciation are justified and thus tax-exempt will not be easy to establish. (We will return to this point.) But as a matter of principle, taxes on income should be paid from actual income and not from capital. The latter circumstance is the case, however, if inflation is not taken into account in calculating depreciation.

---

[1] Not all enterprises are reporting increased depreciation. Here and there depreciation is still calculated on the basis of the same percentage of original book value. This proves that not everyone understands the monetary aspects of depreciation and that inflationary profits are not universally available for subsequent catch-up.

Just as obvious as the need for an increase in annual depreciation is the need for an allowance for these higher depreciation charges in setting prices. Proceeds from sales of goods today occur as paper marks. A businessman who uses past depreciation rates in setting prices realizes them in paper marks and thus places himself in the position of not being able to pay the higher replacement costs of plant assets. The main misgivings regarding the allowance for higher paper-mark depreciation charges in the price formation process include not only the fact that during periods of changing prices future replacement costs may be quite arbitrarily set, but the fact that a tendency may emerge to accelerate the depreciable lives of assets to the greatest extent possible - from twenty years to ten years or even five or three years; in other words, to increase correspondingly the amount of depreciation per year and thus the surcharges for price formation purposes currently. During periods of inflation these increases mean an additional, powerful stimulus for further price increases; a shifting of the components of future prices to goods manufactured currently; an intensification of inflation at the most inauspicious of moments. If there are also businessmen who then add additional surcharges for possible price declines "relative to goods currently in process," for "losses due to a decline in exchange rates," etc., one will no doubt feel compelled to endorse an official audit or other price verification procedure as a matter of principle. On the other hand, prices driven high by this costing process will be even more adversely affected by a downswing in the economy. Ruinous price fluctuations, therefore, are as a rule magnified by such costing behavior.

2. Accounting for depreciation, however, takes on quite a different face during inflation. If as a matter of principle one calculates depreciation on the basis of replacement cost - at present in terms of today's inflated paper marks -, that is, calculates depreciation for the same asset with the same productive capacity and allocates it over the same number of years, always adjusting the amount for changes in the replacement cost of the asset, the gold-mark accounts may soon run out of room for the annual paper-mark depreciation amounts. In our example, the historical cost of the asset was 1,000,000 M., depreciation over six years, 300,000 M., and the book value at the end of 1918, 700,000 M.

A remaining depreciable value of 700,000 M. cannot accommodate annual deprecia-tion of 1,000,000 paper marks (on a replacement value of 20 million marks). This example demonstrates the absurdity of today's customary practice of recognizing paper mark depreciation on low gold-mark values. Paper marks can only be deducted from paper marks. For this reason, depreciation today (paper-mark depreciation) should only be recognized on paper-mark accounts and not on gold-mark accounts. Thus, if restating old gold-mark accounts in terms of paper marks (as explained above) is out of the question, a replacement reserve or, if necessary, a replacement fund should be established. The accounting would appear as follows:

Debit:

   Plant assets

      Book value at end of 1918: 700,000 M.

Credit:

   Replacement reserve

      Depreciation through 1918

      1.   Difference due to inflation for 6 years. The 300,000 M. are to be restated by 5,700,000 M. so that 1,000,000 M. per year for six years will have been accumulated.

      2.   Depreciation for 1919, 1,000,000 M.

The retroactive effect of this procedure on enterprise "profit" will not be pursued here.

Clearly, then, the 6,700,000 M. set aside for replacement, when added to the old accumulated depreciation amount of 300,000 M., make up the necessary amount for 7 years in relation to a replacement cost of 20,000,000 marks depreciated over 20 years. A few firms already account substantially as illustrated above or in a similar manner. The reserves, however, usually appear under such titles as reserve account, special reserve, etc. In any case, the replacement-reserve method is not yet being applied commonly and systematically in German accounting practice. But it is only a question of time before enterprises will make use of it.[2]

If many companies today still shrink from using replacement accounts, especially when it comes to crediting them for the full amount necessary to replace assets, they do so because the tax authorities are wont to construe the larger sums as genuine reserves and thus declare them taxable. Given the great perils enterprises already face because their more or less purely inflationary profits are taxed away, it is a matter of broad general interest that the tax authorities soon recognize the true nature of increased depreciation. At present, widespread aversion to unconcealed replacement reserves results in further distortion of accounting data. Since, as was shown above, most plant asset accounts technically do not permit increased depreciation in paper marks, the bookkeeper looks about for other accounts that could accommodate the extra depreciation; hence the common practice of including reserve accounts among liabilities in order to conceal them. Under certain circumstances, accordingly, sizeable liabilities, which usually are not a good sign financially, represent a financial cushion, that is, plant asset replacement reserves, but only recognizable and knowable as such to the initiated. Above all, inventories, including raw material inventories, goods in process, and finished goods, have to provide content for the balance sheets businessmen want to offer the public and the tax authorities - or can afford to if they have given up hope that the tax authorities will recognize the true nature of increased depreciation. In the abstract, there is no compelling reason during periods of rising prices such as we have just experienced to value inventories, say in the balance sheet at the close of 1919, especially low. Nevertheless, one cannot blame the businessman who at that time allowed for the risk of a price decline by valuing inventories low. But aside from this consideration many enterprises have valued inventories so low - I have this from their reports as well as my own observations - that considerable secret reserves have resulted. Among these secret reserves were those very depreciation allocations that could not be accommodated in the plant asset accounts, but that were not to appear openly as such either. That on occasion asset quantities were not reported in

---

[2]   Individual firms accounted according to the depreciation-reserve method even before the war. Examples include Mechanical Cotton Mill, Augsburg, Cologne-Neuessen Mining Association, Becker Steel Works, A.G.

full in the balance sheet is an open secret. This arose not only because businessmen feared taxation itself, but because they knew or sensed that the tax involved was based on economically untenable principles. If low-priced inventories are sold at higher prices, adequate means for acquiring costly replacements are received. Of course these proceeds appear as profits in the next fiscal year, but initially, at least they function as enterprise working capital. If prices fall, the secret reserves associated with inventory become smaller. At the same time, however, costs of replacements become proportionately smaller as well. As a result of these considerations, the tendency in valuing inventory is more and more to approximate old gold-mark prices. The inventory account in some balance sheets, accordingly, may still be regarded as a gold-mark figure.

With respect to the tax treatment of paper-mark depreciation and reserves, one certainly should not disregard the fact that the effect of inflation, that is, the portion of depreciation and reserves attributable to inflation, cannot be precisely determined. To continue the above example, whether or not the replacement machine actually costs 20 million marks after twenty years or whether or not the assumed useful life of the old machine will actually amount to 20 years cannot be known for sure in advance. In face of all this uncertainty, the businessman will be inclined to take as a basis for depreciation the highest possible replacement cost and the shortest possible useful life so that invested capital is recovered quickly. The tax authorities, on the other hand, may contend that lower prices will be the rule again within a reasonable span of time. One could well say, then, that for every single depreciation charge recognized today differences in opinion may arise as to the extent that it is purely inflationary, is only another numerical expression of its value under stable conditions, or on top of all is a taxable reserve.

But after all is said and done: it is in the general interest of the economy that increases in depreciation due to inflation not be taxed without further ado (the current tax rates not being insignificant). In view of the considerable variability in price changes and the fact that prices continue to change, a more mechanical consideration of the effect of inflation on depreciation and reserves cannot be avoided. Perhaps, depending on the particular assets, one can permit paper-mark depreciation rates six or twelve times previous rates, the rates best being set by a mixed committee of tax officials and businessmen. If the value of money increases appreciably in later years, a re-examination could take place to determine whether or not accumulated depreciation is still greater than replacement cost. If the depreciation amounts at work in the enterprise were not affected by losses due to the downward pressure on prices, a subsequent, additional tax would become a possibility. In light of the uncertain outlook for an improvement in the monetary situation, in any event, I consider it most unfortunate that the tax authorities today allow only a small, totally inadequate increase in depreciation because of inflation.

A second article will consider the effect of inflation on accounting for replacements and acquisitions in the post-war period.

2. Replacements and Acquisitions
During Inflation[*]
Professor W. Prion[1]
Cologne

I.

Prior to the war the rule generally held that upon retirement of a plant asset, accumulated depreciation provided for replacement, and the cost of replacement was charged to the plant and equipment account. The acquisition or reproduction price paid for the replacement asset was substituted for the depreciated balance in the asset account, and depreciation was then recognized on that price. As I explained in my article on depreciation, not only has it proved necessary to increase depreciation charges dramatically as a result of the huge increases in the cost of replacing worn-out plant assets, but depreciation recognized in the past has been undermined by inflation, that is, to the extent it was not invested in raw materials or inventory but remained in paper marks. Thus, as was evident from the example, special reserve allocations are also necessary to increase accumulated depreciation to the paper-mark amount required for replacement. If this state of affairs had been correctly understood by all concerned, neither enterprise owners nor the public would have been so astonished at the "huge" profits of enterprises. Indeed, the hide-and-seek games I described in my article that businessmen played with these profits could have been avoided, and many a dividend policy would have been a different, more prudent one. But since these relationships were not widely understood, a very large number of enterprises has not even provided for increased depreciation and reserves. They have, for example, gotten into a most awkward situation when they accounted as follows:

---

[*] *Plutus*, 27 September 1920, pp. 334-37.

[1] My article concerning depreciation [article no.1] contains a number of printing errors. In particular, lines 10-11 in the second paragraph should read "depreciation was not based simply and purely on replacement cost, ..." Likewise, lines 15-16 in the same paragraph should read "more or less on the basis of actual replacement cost." I would also like to refer the reader to my article on "Depreciation and Taxes" in the *Kölnische Volkszeitung*, 29 September 1920.

Acquisition price, 1 January 1910	1,000,000
Depreciation through 1918	900,000
Book value, 1 January 1919	100,000
Replacement account 1919 (equal to one year's allocation for an antici- pated 20 million marks replacement cost)	2,000,000
Sale of the old asset	2,000,000
Replacement cost, 1 January 1920	20,000,000

On hand are:

Depreciation for 1919		2,000,000
1920 proceeds	2,000,000	
Less book value	− 100,000	1,900,000
Depreciation 1910 through 1918		900,000
		4,800,000

The enterprise, accordingly, is 15,200,000 paper marks short. What the businessman overlooked here is that 17,100,000 marks needed to be set aside over and above the 900,000 marks actually accumulated (18,000,000 paper marks less 900,000 marks), or 15,200,000 marks received over and above the 1,900,000 realized on disposal of the old asset. Since this did not happen, the businessman faces the problem of finding the 15 million marks for replacement. The solution is clear: the replacement cost should have been accumulated automatically from revenues in past years, and the mechanism for doing so is depreciation.

There are several possibilities:

Either: Profit is relatively small and an "appropriate" dividend is paid anyway. (Profit may also be large, in which case large dividends are paid.) In this case, there is no alternative but to raise new capital or to postpone replacement indefinitely "until prices have fallen." Here one should consider the very important fact that no plant expansion or enhancement of functional capacity is associated with the new capital. Rather, the objective is to maintain previous productivity levels by replacing a no longer useful asset with a new one. The additional capital raised, further, will give rise to increased dividend rights if capital stock outstanding is increased, or increased fixed interest payments if debenture capital is increased. Observation indicates that numerous enterprises have found themselves in these circumstances and that many continue to do so.

If new capital is raised, the entry is: plant and equipment + 20 million marks and capital + 20 millions marks. The new plant assets are recorded in paper marks in the plant and equipment account and appear as such in the balance sheet, unless in that particular year substantial revenues permit immediate write-downs to pre-war prices (e.g., 1 million, which has the character of a gold-mark value).

Other enterprises, given the high costs of new plant assets and the difficulty of raising capital, will have attempted to postpone replacement again and again. These "attempts" have now spread over almost five years; they are based on the hope that prices will finally start to fall. Experts say that this policy of making do and biding one's time has led to serious deterioration of plant and equipment in many firms and may continue for some time. Since a truly perceptible rise in the value of money, that is, a price decline, does not appear imminent - (financial terms of peace!) - and since plant asset replacement cannot be postponed indefinitely, the consequences of inflation as described here will make themselves felt even more strongly, and certainly so if the difficulties associated with raising capital do not abate.

Or: Enterprises have at their disposal adequate paper-mark profits from which depreciation and reserve allocations proportional to replacement costs can be taken. In this case, the procedure (using the same example) would be:

Deductions from profit:

Depreciation for 1919	2,000,000 M.
Additional charge to compensate for depreciation from 1910 to 1918 (which amounted to only 900,000 M.) if compensation has not already taken place or no reserve is available	17,100,000 M.
So that profit is reduced by	19,100,000 M.,

and a reserve in that amount is created. When the reserve is created, further, the plant and equipment account is debited for the 900,000 M. depreciation previously recognized so that 20 million marks are available for replacement. If the 20 million M. are disbursed, the replacement account is debited and 1 million marks, the original peace-time price, remains in the plant and equipment account. If one wished to state the account in paper marks, and thus the plant assets at their replacement cost in the balance sheet, a credit to a capital account on the right hand side of the balance sheet corresponding to the increase in the plant and equipment account on the left hand side should be made as follows:

Plant and equipment   19,000,000
            Capital appreciation   19,000,000

This clear and manifest treatment of replacements during inflation, however, has not found widespread application, not, at least, as far as I can judge from published balance sheets. More popular, because easier and more secretive, is the practice of simply taking the cost of replacements from profit and only charging to the plant and equipment account an amount approximating the pre-war cost. The effect is the same. The problem with this practice is that the tax authorities will not be so easily convinced that the expenditures are for replacements, which, as explained above, should be exempt from tax as a matter of principle.

II.

So much for replacements. It is a different matter with actual additions, with expenditures intended to improve, augment, or expand plant facilities. As was explained in some detail above in relation to depreciation, any additional expense incurred in acquiring replacement plant and equipment, to the extent it applies to plant expansion or enhancement of productive capacity, is as a matter of principle to be paid from new capital. This stipulation is especially true for funds expended for obvious expansions or augmentations of plant facilities, for new buildings, new machines, or new installations that have a useful life longer than one year. These expenditures should be charged to the plant and equipment account. They not only represent expenditures chargeable to the year in which they occurred, but to all subsequent years in which they are productive. Expenditures for additions, then, decrease annual profit only as a result of the year's pro rata share of depreciation. They appear as a part of the balance in the plant and equipment account until their final disposition. This is true from the standpoint of business economics and in tax law.

Yet before the war many firms showed a tendency to book outlays for such long-lived plant expansion - whether in full or in more or less large part (depending on the amount) - as a period cost, that is, to charge them to profit and loss rather than plant and equipment. The use of earned surplus for plant expansion purposes ("capitalization of earnings" in technical terms) was even considered a very sound means of financing and was widely recommended for joint-stock companies, although the earnings of joint-stock companies actually ought to be distributed to shareholders. A good example of this practice is Bochum Cast Steel whose management financed two thirds of its entire plant out of earned surplus prior to the outbreak of hostilities.

Regarding this financing and accounting practice, however, it should be noted that enterprises generally paid for new buildings, acquisitions, and plant expansion from surplus already on hand and avoided charging the outlays to the cost of plant assets. Thus, it did not matter whether or not the surplus had arisen during the current year or was available in the form of open or secret reserves that stemmed from prior years. In highly unusual cases, cost-based prices may have been increased from the outset by the amount of the outlay for the planned additions. The sharp competition in almost every market, however, usually resulted in the adaptation of cost calculations to market prices. The thinking in the case of capitalized earnings, on the other hand, was to obtain a more favorable cost basis for goods manufactured (by minimizing depreciation) and at the same time to hold down capital entitled to dividends or interest. Of course every enterprise sought to realize, quite independently of its cost accounting, the highest possible prices and the highest possible profits, the latter making the method of financing possible in the first place.

In today's inflationary environment new plant and equipment costs huge sums of paper marks. For this reason, enterprises are reluctant to invest in new plant facilities unless they have ample profits available which they do not wish to hand over to others. Even repairs and maintenance of existing plant and equipment, which was under great strain but neglected during the war and much of which is on the brink of falling apart, require huge sums of money; to the extent, that is, that maintenance is possible given the shortage of certain raw materials and factory supplies. In any case, additions and repairs are so costly today that they cause the businessman a great deal of concern.

At present, enterprises are again very much inclined to charge off (depending on their size) the cost of additions immediately, that is, to charge them against profit for the year, even though additions unquestionably represent an expansion of the firm and contribute to increased production for years. Businessmen are reluctant to record and carry forward from year to year new plant costs that are so incredibly high compared to the gold-mark amounts of old plant and equipment still on the books. In addition, the increased paper-money revenues and surpluses that result from ongoing inflation are reported as accounting profit, the size of which in relation to paid-in capital - paid-in capital generally having been paid for in gold marks - arouses feelings of unease. For these reasons businessmen rush to use increased paper-money revenues to pay for new plant and equipment, especially since they do not know whether or not they will be able to raise funds for it otherwise (bank credits, issuance of stock or bonds).

Apart from the disadvantage to shareholders who receive the same or only a slightly higher dividend on their gold-mark investment, the practice of financing new plant and equipment from earned surplus is, from the standpoint of the enterprise, absolutely correct. Its financial position is strengthened. But it also illustrates how private interests and the interest of the economy often conflict. Namely, the payment of new plant costs out of current net income can lead the businessman to incorporate these costs in *toto* in the prices of the goods he produces. Given the condition of most of today's markets, the shortages and consequent opportunities to increase prices, it is not difficult to raise commodity prices by the amount of these outlays. Raising commodity prices by this amount, in turn, means that plant assets whose cost should be charged to a series of annual net incomes, are charged to the current year's net income. The result, as was already shown to be the case when excessive depreciation was recognized on old assets, in that the overburdened present also has to bear the cost of plant assets that only become fully productive in the future. The right must be reserved for national economic policymakers to establish a balance between the interests of enterprises and the interest of the general public.

Usually, however, high paper-mark profits during inflation are not sufficient to cover the cost of new plant assets. The common complaint on the part of enterprises is that even when additions are limited to those absolutely necessary, raising new capital to cover their cost cannot be avoided. But when new plant assets are purchased with new capital, the tendency immediately to write off a large amount of the cost charged to the plant and equipment account still prevails.

In following these accounting and costing policies, the businessman assumes that price developments in the future are uncertain and above all that a general decline in prices may occur. In the latter case, he believes, recognizing high depreciation charges on assets acquired at high prices is not feasible, that is, it jeopardizes the profitability of his enterprise. The businessman who advocates such prudence, however, frequently overlooks the fact that although a decline in prices diminishes revenues (sales remaining constant), enterprise expenditures diminish as well. In particular, the costs of replacements fall, and with them depreciation charges. In addition, during periods of falling prices or monetary appreciation previously accumulated depreciation gains purchasing power if it is on hand in the form of money or monetary claims, and not invested in nonmonetary assets - raw materials, finished goods - subject to ongoing loss of value. To be sure, high paper-mark book values may remain on the books as residual amounts in such a case. They will, however, have lost value in a general price decline.[2] Thus, the balance sheet is subject to the opposite effect as was the case under ongoing inflation. The losses may be offset in the books by debiting the capital appreciation account if one was created; otherwise, one may charge them to other reserves, or, as a last resort, one may write down share capital. (It becomes clear here how mistaken it is to regard excess revenues realized under conditions of accelerating inflation as pure profit, or worse, to treat them as such.) Even if the businessman makes a good faith effort to put these considerations into practice, he does not relish the difficulties, the uncertainties, the confusion, the backwards and forwards changes in the capital accounts. It is simply easier to write down the total cost

---

[2]   Example:

Acquisition 1920	20,000,000 M.
Accumulated depreciation 1920	2,000,000 M.
Book value 1921	18,000,000 M.

In 1921 the machine costs only one half its original price. Annual depreciation, therefore, becomes one million marks. Nine years later total depreciation amounts to 11 million marks, which covers replacement cost. The residual book value is 7 million marks, which represents the loss in real value.

of plant assets (or a large portion thereof) to their pre-war prices immediately. Besides, the practice seems natural enough since it undoubtedly promotes the well-being of the enterprise. But the businessman chooses the well-being of his enterprise over economy-wide considerations. For this reason, price control boards, as agents of the national economy, may become necessary to prevent transformation of caution on the part of the businessman - caution that is entirely appropriate from a business economics point of view - into a major price escalation.

3. Economic Relativity[*]

Walter Mahlberg

Munich

The confusion of economic concepts among the public is gradually taking on such grotesque dimensions that a consideration of the very foundations of our economic existence appears necessary.

I. Inflation and Its Scope

Before the war we lived in "good circumstances." In 1914 Germany's assets comprised its land, the natural resources above and below the earth, buildings, tools, machines, furnishings, equipment, streets, canals, railroad tracks, vehicles, and stocks of inventories in all commercial, agricultural, public and private businesses. In addition, we owned assets in the colonies and abroad as well as foreign receivables (foreign securities, bills receivable, etc.). If we deducted our foreign debts, what remained was Germany's wealth as of 1 August 1914.

The value of domestic shares, bonds, bills, notes, savings deposits and the like is a transitory item that is always counter-balanced since one party to such a contract is always a debtor and the other a creditor, each for the same amount. If we prepared the same balance sheet today, we would see that our net worth has not increased on the whole, as was the case for year after year before the war, but in fact has dwindled away considerably. The earth has been plundered, natural resources have suffered uneconomical exploitation, all plant, installations, and equipment are in total disrepair as they have not been adequately "refurbished," and, above all, the necessities of life have been exhausted, right down to the last crate of merchandise and the house-wife's last patching rag. If we measure our losses by the peace treaty, by the reduction in our manpower, and by the destruction of the value of our companies overseas, we see how much smaller the worth of our net assets is now relative to 1914. In contrast to this impoverishment, ownership of receivables and securities of every description by individuals and the population in general

---

[*] *Zeitschrift für Handelswissenschaft- und Handelspraxis*, 1920, pp. 133-6, 182-86, and 195-97.

has ballooned into many, many billions of notes and savings and bank deposits. One need only think of the 100 billion marks in war bonds outstanding.

To fully grasp the concept of inflation (*inflatio, Aufblähung, Aufgeblasenheit*), which is beginning to appear, though not all that clearly, we must understand how our wealth in 1914 became the poverty of today. The economic objective of our lives, whether we be doctor, actor, bureaucrat or laborer, merchant, farmer, etc., consists in keeping the German economic system running in such a productive way that

1. it produces enough food, clothing, accommodation, health, recreation, etc., for everyone;

2. it operates at full capacity; and

3. it constantly expands so that wealth expands.

Every profession is equally important in this output process. Although the work of one profession might seem more essential than another, we cannot simply say that one is more productive and the other "unproductive" (or only indirectly productive). Nevertheless, one can assert unconditionally, and this is conceptually correct, that work (or the related expenditure) that is not "proportional" to the greater output described above, that is, where expenditure is greater than output, is unproductive; for the concept of economic efficiency requires that output be greater than expenditure if the wealth mentioned in no. 3 above is to materialize.

As far as I can see, one cannot say without reservation which particular expenditures are unproductive when uneconomical conditions prevail. Thus, the following proposition represents only a schematic illustration of the relativity at issue. If total revenue increases, so, too, can the number of actors, bureaucrats, etc.; if total revenue decreases, as is the case today compared to 1914, the number of actors and bureaucrats should also decrease if expenditures for them are not to be unproductive. Should total wealth not increase (no. 3), or should the status quo not be maintained (no. 2), or should the needs of no. 1 no longer be completely met, then the amount of unproductive work or related expenditures increases, any assumptions regarding their appropriateness notwithstanding. More and more previously productive work is becoming unproductive. Since 1914 we have lived terribly unproductively: we have spent a great deal and achieved nothing more but to have lived so much the worse the longer we live. There is no question of growth or maintenance of wealth. Well-nourished, well-clothed and well-equipped people not only failed to produce anything, they dutifully did the opposite. Production itself was even partly unproductive (munitions, for example). Yesterday's enemy, France, for example, has capitalized this same unproductive expense as war profit and hopes that we realize it. In this regard the value of France's currency depends in part on the value of our own.

At first we could allow ourselves the luxury of living in this manner since our circumstances were good. We could afford it. But we gave it away, not as a gift or without cost, but in exchange for war debt. The increase in the war debt, despite the fact that the value behind it exploded like shrapnel in the air, meant relative inflation - but not for the whole amount. In part the fruit described in no. 1 above was borne, and for a short while we could allow ourselves this luxury without any profound effect or without its becoming immediately unproductive, for example, if the war had turned into nothing but a general manoeuvre.

The inflationary effect increased as the carrying capacity of the economy diminished. After the armistice, unproductive military expenditures waned with demobilization. In their place appeared another type of unproductive outlay and along with it reduced output, which amounts to the same thing in the end. The reduction of the work day to eight hours (despite the fact that before the war, when the economy was stronger, more working hours were necessary to prevent the comforts of life from becoming unproductive expense), days lost to revolution and strikes (which are comparable to days lost to war), stipends for families of the war dead and for disabled veterans, increases in unproductive government institutions, the inability to curb our appetite for the pleasures of life, and last but not least the so-called reduction in the prices of foodstuffs by means of government subsidies, led to an ever weaker carrying capacity of the entire economy, and inflation accelerated, presumably in a progressive manner.

The comparison of the situation in 1914 to the situation today explains the inflationary impoverishment that becomes apparent as to cause but not extent. The extent of inflation cannot of course be determined, although we can probably demonstrate negatively how great it is not. The consequence of nonproductivity and the exhaustion of inventories is a shortage of everything. Yet the buying power of the population has not decreased proportionately given military retirement stipends, compulsory payments for strike days, unemployment benefits, the proliferation of bureaucrats, etc. The result is a rise in the price level, and, as Professor Walb has shown in nos. 275 and 280 of the *Kölnische Zeitung*, in the exchange rate, with foreign goods now commanding great sums of marks.

The turnover of goods with a unit price of 60 M. requires six times the currency than for the turnover of the same goods when they only cost 10 M. Correspondingly, the value of certain possessory rights has risen, for example, the amount of bills receivable drawn against goods, the net proceeds of mined coal, labor earnings, etc. That notes in circulation and cash on hand had to be increased to colossal proportions because of these two phenomena is not inflation, which is what concerns us here. If in 1914 the government had waved a magic wand and there had been a tenfold rise overnight in all ratios expressed in marks (including the marks minted from 1 kg of gold), then the overall situation would not have changed; the only necessary change would have been in the foreign exchange rate, such as the French franc of 81 M. to 810 M. at home and 123.45 F. to 12.35 F. abroad. In the 27 March 1920 issue of the *Münchener Neueste Nachrichten* a member of the Currency Commission wrote that the domestic bank note circulation is estimated at only 26 billion, that is, half of the total bank notes and treasury notes issued and six times the amount of peacetime circulation. Of the other half, approximately 18 billion were floating overseas and around 8 billion were being hoarded from fear of taxation and the future. Disregarding the matter of estimative accuracy, these figures are only an illustration of the above exposition; they say nothing of the extent of inflation. For yet a further relativity must be considered, that is, that fewer sales due to increases in unit prices moderate increases in total sales.

Nothing more can be said about the extent of inflation. It is relative in all directions. How can goiter be cured? The phenomenon is similar to a joint-stock company that reports open reserves, while the book values of its assets are carried too high. The amounts can be written down on both sides and thus the correct relationship reestablished, although doing so will not bring back society's wasted assets. Correspondingly, the Reich could call in large amounts of notes or loans as property tax levies and extinguish the total amount of the debt. Perhaps this would have an effect on the prices of goods and labor and not on unproductively employed items since once something is vainly blown apart it does not come back to life by expropriating the suppliers. The goiter, or, better, the lesion in the economic corpus, is exactly like the joint-stock company; the body can become so strong through diligence and economy that earlier dissipation becomes less and less perceptible. As regards the state or its citizenry, on the other hand, the enormous war debt represents a case of true revolutionary profiteering, for its effect is to spirit away property from owners. In terms of the value of a labor hour, the enormous war debt of the Reich hardly amounts to the few billion in pre-war Reich loans, which are scarcely worth a few pitiful million today. If the equivalent of 100 M. in war loans was 10 working days, today it is barely worth two. Or if in the past one could buy 30 pounds of margarine for a certain amount, the same amount today can only buy three and one-third pounds. From the standpoint of national financial policy (and the citizens who have to pay back these loans as debtors) this represents a huge relief and provides an explanation for the relatively favorable exchange rate - and this quite apart from the fact that it brands the idea of national bankruptcy due to the war debt a farce. For those adversely affected by this phenomenon, which also applies to the purchasing power of interest, it represents an expropriation compared to which the Reich emergency tax pales in significance. Indeed, there are those who view this development (which in the end traces to price controls) as public fraud. I will discuss the damage to the public in this regard below. Rather than healing the wounds of inflation, moreover, this expropriatory process represents an enormous shift in the war burden away from those without any property.[1]

Now that this pseudo healing process of the goiter of the past has taken place, we can drop the concept of inflation and instead speak clearly and in plain German about impoverishment as a result of "shameful squandering." Perhaps that would better help us put a stop to these unproductive outlays, to today's and tomorrow's wastefulness. Is this goiter going to continue to sprout like weeds? Are we going to continue to manage the economy unproductively as described above? Here, too, there is a kind of pseudo healing: decreases in productivity, continued pursuit of luxury, increases in expenditures for public

---

[1]   For details concerning inflation, see Prion, *Inflation und Geldentwertung*, Berlin 1919.

officials in the broadest sense (ministers, officials, veterans' associations, veterans' affairs offices, municipal authorities, shop councils, workers' councils, executive committees, registry functionaries, usury offices, etc.), - all of which ought to be brought into relationship with the already greatly reduced carrying capacity of the economy - do not appear unproductive to full effect since people scrimp and save for the cost of these hard-won achievements. People are prepared to pay dearly for rights in the decision-making process: instead of stripping down to one's underwear, that is, to the bare essentials, and nourishing the body, the honorable citizenry works on squaring the circle, trying to spirit back lost prosperity by further unproductive outlays, or, in today's terminology, by "organizing it back."

In the long run this will not work. It is not possible to drop below a certain level of physical well-being nor to remove the last stitch, etc.; for as soon as there is no more scrimping and saving, the pleasure the citizenry takes in political achievements becomes truly unproductive and continues at the expense of whatever assets may be left and thus at the cost of further general impoverishment. A communistic restructuring of property rights could not prevent this from happening. Since production grows each day, we can sustain these democratic, utopian ideals more and more easily. Unfortunately, however, the expression "more and more easily" can be understood only in relative terms. Considered in the absolute, these things, as demonstrated below, are economically impossible given the burden of our impoverishment since 1914. They represent genuinely unproductive outlays, genuine, ongoing inflation, and the continuation of the wasteful war economy. If the wastefulness of the war economy was justified politically on the basis of the exigencies of war, then today's wastefulness may be explained by the exigencies of the domestic situation - but not when one considers our impoverishment and war losses. Before I go into this issue and the role of the exchange rate, I want to touch on several private-sector consequences, after which I shall once again emphasize that the spread of inflation may be prevented not by reducing the number of bank notes issued, but (1) absolutely by saving and (2) relatively by increasing labor productivity.

II. Effects of Inflation on Private Enterprises

In the private sector there are many parallels that clarify the overall situation. When we examine fixed asset values in the balance sheets of joint-stock companies for instance, land, buildings, equipment and tools usually represent "pre-war goods" valued at "pre-war prices." They surely therefore represent gold marks and contain an enormous "secret reserve" in terms of today's prices. The presence of these reserves explains why the upsurge in equity prices continued uninterrupted, unlike what is happening to the prices of government securities, bonds, indeed, all funds. The shareholder is owner of these actual goods, the bondholder merely a creditor, only an owner of marks receivable, the value of which melts away with inflation. If 50% of the assets of a joint-stock company was necessary to cover a bond debt in 1914, today we would need only 10%, perhaps 5% of the same fixed asset values of the same company to cover the same debt, which indicates that the physical property of the shareholders in terms of these assets has grown from 50% to 90 or 95%. The relationship between homeowners and mortgagors will become the same. In spite of this, one hardly need envy the shareholders, especially when one considers that

1. due to equity prices which have now risen several hundred per cent[2] companies have to offer many times the amount of previous dividends, say 15, 20, 30%, in order to yield a return for the shareholder as great as, for example, from a war loan, and that

2. companies are partially in the position to do so due to the relatively greater productivity of their fixed assets (in reality a mere illusion) and because profits have kept pace with the increased prices of goods.

Apart from the fact that official price controls are choking the growth of profits with might and main, it is not really a question of wealth accumulation in the case of the shareholders, but of the same relentless impoverishment that affects everyone and that will continue to affect everyone. To be exact, it is a matter of inflation in the private sector,

---

[2] For additional information, see Hertlein, "Einfluß von Änderungen des Geldwertes auf den Wert der Aktien" (The influence of changes in the value of money on the value of equity securities), 1920, in no. 4 of this journal.

inflation in the sense of unproductive activity. For receiving a dividend is not what is important; more important is maintaining the existence of the enterprise itself.

The existence of individual businesses is threatened in that state price controls force them to sell their products and services not based on cost of reproduction, but at historical cost plus profit. To begin with, because of the cost component, "depreciation," this situation has an effect on enterprise fixed assets. The economic significance of depreciation becomes clear when one considers that enterprise capital may be subject to three situations in the bookkeeping sense. Capital can

1. be increased by additional contributions or accumulation of profits,

2. be decreased by capital repayments or operating losses, or

3. be maintained at the same level.

The economic process for the third possibility is asset replacement, that is, the maintenance of the status quo in productive capacity. The costs necessary for maintaining productive capacity must be accumulated and borne by the consumer just as the costs of wages and materials are. The essential part of productive-capacity maintenance costs arises from the gradual consumption of assets, which, when worn out must be replaced. Total consumption usually lasts a number of years. Thus, one generally works with annual depreciation quotas based on historical cost. These quotas, in turn, provide a standard measure for yearly, daily, hourly, or per unit costs of consumption.

If one measures these quotas so that useful life, historical cost, and accumulated depreciation articulate, then everything in pre-war times was in order; capital, in terms of bookkeeping, was neither decreased nor increased, but was maintained and the accumulated quotas were sufficient for the acquisition of replacements and renewals. On the bookkeeping side of things nothing has changed, of course. Only the quotas determined on the basis of pre-war prices are no longer sufficient to replace machinery and the like despite the fact that enterprise capital is maintained at the same level. The quotas, and thus the depreciation cost charged, ought to be increased to such an extent that their accumulated amount suffices to acquire machinery, etc., at today's enormously inflated prices. In bookkeeping terms this is not maintenance of capital, but augmentation of capital. It is, however, capital growth in the bookkeeping sense only. The assets of the business - what it owns - are not increased in this manner. Rather, the status quo is merely maintained. By comparison assets are decreased when one bases depreciation on historical values rather than future values. The businessman becomes poorer, and not only in theory, but in fact; for the matter also applies to values with shorter useful lives, particularly all maintenance and repair costs. Although Professor Schmalenbach of the University of Cologne explained this a year ago[3] and more recently in a different connection,[4] his former colleague, Undersecretary of State Julius Hirsch, has disallowed the coal-mining industry an increase in coal prices to cover current costs. His argument is that the general public should not be burdened with creating private business capital. But this process creates neither public nor private capital, only abstract, bookkeeping capital. The mining industry simply wants to avoid general impoverishment. If, from an economy-wide point of view, the effect were such a self-serving one, it would be difficult to face up to envious people. Besides, the effect on the economy is not that inflation would increase by these amounts, for inflation means asset consumption, living off capital instead of interest. This latter effect is caused largely by price controls which push prices below replacement costs. It is just another guise of inflation. This erosion of other people's asset base, whether they are factory owners or farmers, together with the aforementioned profligate spending at the expense of the citizenry, makes possible the unproductive wasteful expenditures discussed above.

The existence of businesses, whether large or small, is threatened from yet another direction. If a retail business is to function properly, it requires a correspondingly "assorted" inventory. Nowadays the shop shelves are alarmingly empty, display windows are furnished with dummies. Yet the value of this greatly reduced and sadly insufficient stock of goods is the same as before, or even greater thanks to alleged war profits - all of which is as much an oracle as the Sibylline Books, except that the process continues inexorably and will soon include shops that appear relatively full today. The merchant becomes poorer, even though he maintains his taxable base or perhaps even increases it;

---

[3] *Grundlagen dynamischer Bilanzlehre* [Dynamic accounting], 1919.
[4] "Selbstkostenrechnung" [Cost accounting], Part 1. This article and the article cited in note 3 appeared in *Zeitschrift für handelswissenschaftliche Forschung*, Vol. 13.

for afterwards, "when there are plenty of goods again," that base will only amount to a pittance. Joint-stock companies, who have also fallen prey to the same misfortune in regard to supplies, raw materials, labor, and finished goods appear to be able to resolve the problem by issuing new shares of stock. And the financial columns in the newspapers are brimming with advertisements for subscription offers. Apart from the facts that a single proprietorship may raise new capital as well and that a joint-stock company has many owners instead of one, this pseudosolution is illustrated by the following example from the *Münchener Neueste Nachrichten* of 25 March 1920.

According to this example, the operation of the largest Augsburg cotton mill is running at only 20% of its capacity. Instead of 2,800 bales of cotton per month only 500 bales are used and a corresponding stock is kept. If the mill were to return to full productivity, it would require an inventory worth 100 million just for raw materials in terms of today's cotton prices, and this alongside a share capital of around 4 million. These figures ought to speak to even the cleverest party functionary. The faster the artisan, shopkeeper, and manufacturer turns over his inventory, the less likely he is to become impoverished; the older the goods or prices at which he is compelled to sell, the smaller his asset base becomes, the smaller his purchasing power in the future becomes. And the concept of usury is not at all clear any more. Indeed, its socio-juridical relativity ought to be reversed. The primary production and service sectors (e.g., banks) suffer least from this "erosion of assets through profitable turnover."[5]

As a by-product of massive infusions of capital, joint-stock companies have managed to water down their dividends. For this reason, their shareholders avoid the high, pre-war progressive tax rates on nominal dividends, which today are simply not justifiable. On the other hand, these infusions of capital cannot save joint-stock companies from being acquired by foreign interests in the long run. As shown in the following table, the force of facts is too great.

---

[5]   See also Ludwig Klein, "Der Einfluß der sinkenden Kaufkraft des Geldes auf Kalkulation, Bilanz und Steuer" [The influence of the falling purchasing power of money on cost accumulation, accounting, and taxation], no. 1 of the *Zeitschrift für Handelswissenschaft- und Handelspraxis*, 1920; also Erwin Geldmacher, "Bilanzsorgen" [Accounting problems], *Industrie- und Handelszeitung*, Berlin 1920, nos. 57-63.

	Pre-War Prices	Sale Prices
Mining Share:	(highest rate 1913)	(February 1913)
	1.7 marks = 1 Dutch guilder	35 marks = 1 guilder
Graf Bismark	66,500 = 38,500	138,000 = 3,943
Ewald	48,000 = 28,235	120,000 = 3,430
Lothringen	31,300 = 18,400	108,000 = 3,086
Neustaβfurt	11,900 = 7,000	56,000 = 1,600

(etc., according to a table of an Amsterdam bank, reported in the *Münchener Neueste Nachrichten*)

The inventory situation in Germany is by and large a reflection of our impoverishment, which was discussed in detail above and whose elements are touched upon here. Inasmuch as our impoverishment has already set in, we must come to terms with it. Indeed, we must resign ourselves to its progression as long as the majority of citizens thinks it best that everyone lives - by means of price controls - at the expense of those who still have property. This is the abstract parallel to the concrete idea of the petty revolutionary. We could let things simply run their course if it were not for yesterday's enemy and the exchange rate. If, on the other hand, one reads the Hirsch Memorandum of the State Ministry for Economic Affairs on capital formation and capital procurement, one becomes completely exasperated. Hirsch wants to confiscate private-sector capital which is formed under the adverse conditions described above as a defense mechanism against asset erosion and impoverishment as if owners had no right to it. He wants to transform it into public capital and put it to "nationally productive" use, "as there is a reluctance to invest." The weekly journal of the German Social Democrats *Die neue Zeit* describes the Hirsch plan as a reprisal against the capital strike. It is clearly a consequence of the economically intolerable thought of profiteering.

But the economic confusion in the memorandum goes even further in that it approves of a proposal whereby the authorities raise rentals by 20% and use resulting profits for the construction of public apartment buildings. In this way inevitable increases in prices are to be partially anticipated and "the amounts used productively for the common good rather than just going up in smoke in rivalrous competition, sumptuous living, and capital flight abroad." So many reasons, so many improbabilities. Furthermore, Hirsch plans to use the rent increase that landlords need to cover the prohibitive increases in maintenance costs to build public housing for others. The Babylonian confusion could be no worse.

III. The Amortization of War Losses

Another question is how the deficit resulting from comparing balance sheets from 1914 with those of today can be removed. The loss of areas that are especially important economically magnifies the effect of this deficit to an almost intolerable degree. Disregard for the moment any reparations payments. Before the war the fruit of our labor was sufficient to

1. satisfy the needs of the general population,

2. replace plant and equipment as needed and thus maintain it, and

3. expand plant and equipment to meet the requirements of a growing population and its needs.

To some extent our production apparatus was already spreading abroad. Foreign assets fell into German hands, and in part exports compensated for the large population growth in the sense that we performed work that foreigners would have done or that otherwise would not have been done. Whether our expansion abroad increased or reduced the standard of living of these foreigners is another relativity.

To cover the deficit, we will have to draw on all three of the following sources of revenues

1. The population must be content with less.

2. Nonessential plant and equipment must no longer be maintained.

3. Population growth must be degressive in the future and the upward trend in [the demand for] life's necessities will have to level off, effectively fall, and come into line with point 1.

All of this may not be enough. The spread of our production apparatus abroad, the acquisition of foreign assets, was for the most part only possible because we gave value in the form of our mineral resources in return. It is no coincidence that Alsace-Lorraine, the Saar, and parts of Silesia have been taken from us. We have not only lost the wealth of these regions, but we have to buy it back with the sweat of our brow to the extent that we consume it ourselves (that is, that we do not re-export it). We must also buy back the agricultural surplus of the areas we lost to Poland.

Whether, given the high level of our social outlay, we earned something as a nation from the labor we invested in our goods is not absolutely clear. We did earn something from the fruits of our intellectual and economic culture. Since people abroad experienced the latter aspect of our culture in particular as Prussianism, the export of our labor may be characterized as disadvantageous to their standard of living. For the standard applied here is one established by foreigners and not the standard relationship of work to pleasure that used to prevail in the Ruhr or in Berlin. There is no doubt that foreigners, by way of peace treaties, trade agreements, and tariff policies, will ensure that we get the unpleasant, less profitable work and wrangle for themselves the more pleasant and productive work. On the other hand, our social outlay has grown to gigantic proportions, and far and wide, people are amusing themselves by dismantling our intellectual and economic culture while, like the lucky devil himself, they speak of great achievements. Our enemies, neutral foreign countries, and we ourselves are working with a united front to structure our labor as forced labor for the benefit of these foreign countries. In any event, our deficit will not be so easily amortized by labor.

This fact becomes clearer still if we look at the issue more concretely. Our impoverishment manifests itself in the run-down condition of all our plant and equipment, e.g., our railway system, in the great absence of our inventories, and in our general malnutrition. To close these gaps again, we need, as people are wont to say lightly, raw materials from abroad. We can only acquire foreign goods:

1. if we send our own goods beyond our borders;

2. if foreign countries lend us their goods (against open credit, bills of exchange, private or public bonds, mortgages, and sundry other types of notes), or

3. if foreign countries assume ownership of our domestic assets.

The most convenient way for foreigners to assume ownership of our assets is to acquire share capital. Under the very favorable conditions of pre-war times and before we had lost our valuable mineral resources, the fruit of our labor provided us with sufficient stocks of inventories to trade for the foreign goods we needed. We could even lend part of our income or use it to acquire foreign assets. But even if our current productivity were sufficient to satisfy our ongoing demand for foreign goods, nothing would be left over to close the gaps we have spoken of. The necessary replenishment of inventories, renovation and restoration of plant and equipment, and proper nourishment of man and beast can only be accomplished by means of credit or if foreign countries assume ownership of German property. The scope of this proposition can only be underestimated, not overestimated. Whether credit or property, the yield on the assets and the interest on the credit will flow back to the foreign countries without our receiving any value in return. This is a more concrete expression for the enforced labor described above.

The belief that these foreign credits and ownership rights could gradually be extinguished by means of hard work and frugality evidences another relativity of price controls. With the current exchange rate in Zurich of 10 F. = 100 M., anyone buying, say, 10 F. of Swiss goods on credit and earning 20 M. a day would have to work five days to pay for the transaction. If this person's earnings rose to 100 M. a day because price controls were relaxed, he would only have to work one day to pay for the same transaction, that is, as long as the exchange rate did not deteriorate at the same time. He would only experience a loss if the exchange rate fell below 2 F. = 100 M.

If, for the sake of simplicity, we describe this rate as an "equilibrium rate," we can say the following: as long as the exchange rate does not fall below this equilibrium rate due to relaxation of price controls, the foreign goods acquired on credit to replenish our inventories, etc., can be paid for with a lesser amount of domestic labor than is presently the case. The same applies to the reparations denominated in gold marks we are to pay our enemies. If price controls continue to exist, they will amount to more in terms of German labor than would be the case under a free economy. Indeed, with regard to the transfer of German wealth abroad, relaxing price controls would have a twofold effect: the values of goods already under foreign control would participate in the advantage to be had, and a larger quantity of foreign goods could be obtained for goods yet to be transferred abroad. This situation is the basis for the well-known phenomenon that these days our goods are dumped abroad at rock-bottom sale prices far below the value of the labor contained in them, even when a much heralded, but in reality ridiculous, foreign currency premium of 100% is added to the mark price. The best example is the mining-share table reproduced above. One share represents the value of the labor required to earn a piece of the mine. For a Graf Bismark share a Dutchman once had to pay 38,500 fl. Today he only has to earn 3,900 fl. to become a shareholder.

The crux of the matter is the behaviour of the exchange rate and whether the exchange rate closely follows domestic price developments and would fall as low as the "equilibrium rate" - or even lower - or whether it would not fall so low and still allow us the above cited advantages. The equilibrium rate in the example was set at 2 francs. But it is not at all uniform; it is different for each buyer and fluctuates with the exchange rate. It depends on how closely the price of the object in question approximates its free-market price. In a word, it is no absolute, uniform figure, but a function of multiplicity of relationships. And since there is only one exchange rate for a foreign country and, possibly due to the effect of arbitrage, only one single exchange rate for a national economy with respect to all foreign countries, the manner in which relaxation of price controls will affect the exchange rate is clear.

The majority of citizens generally imagines that some unknown big brother, or, as they say in Bavaria, the *Großkopfete* [rich and powerful] will be called upon to pay the reparations to our former enemies. The most unnecessary clause in the peace treaty stipulates that tax rates in Germany remain extremely high. Economically, the reparations payments are such that German goods will flow abroad, or foreigners will become the owners of German property in Germany itself. We have already seen that our labor output is not enough to keep us healthy and to replenish our inventories and that for this reason large amounts of assets already have to be handed over. If one adds to this trade imbalance the reparations demands of unbelievable billions and huge payments in kind in addition, it becomes clear that the German exchange rate will be under continual pressure for decades, that there will hardly be enough income left after taxes for stale bread and water and that - and it all boils down to this - huge amounts of German property will fall into foreign hands.

How this will take place is totally irrelevant. Perhaps the citizenry will be forced to sell its property to pay taxes or for other reasons. Perhaps company shares will leave the country (or general directors, deputy managers, and boards of directors will "immigrate"). Perhaps government property will become the outright property of enemy governments or the private property of foreigners abroad. Only a miracle can prevent us from becoming a country dominated by foreign proprietors and foreigners from taking our lucrative jobs.

No only will we have to skimp, we will also have to divest ourselves of all our museums along with the museum personnel. Their value probably accounts for only a small fraction of the sum in question. Or maybe we can come closer to covering the sum by transforming our railroads into a joint-stock company and selling the shares abroad.[6]

All this is not just a suggestion, but an illustration of the actual situation. The trust bank proposed by Hirsch that would buy option rights or property in danger of being acquired by foreign interests using the export industry's exchange rate "profits," is as unrealistic as a sand dam built by children at low tide to hold back the high tide, and this quite apart from the fact that these supposed profits are available for this purpose neither from a private enterprise point of view nor from an economy-wide one. We are going to have to formulate economic policy on a grand scale, especially since the peace treaty is designed to protect the interests of the Entente. Which domestic values will be affected first? Where does the internationalization of property ownership do the least damage? Which losses will prove most harmful to our culture? Should we protect companies with large numbers of employees or small? Should we protect urban or rural property? Should foreigners have the right to buy up tracts of land at will, possibly whole adjacent blocks, or should we only make land available in a checker-board pattern? (Of course a "trust bank" would serve to effect the necessary domestic restructuring of the land made

---

[6]   The fact that we would have to acquire foreign exchange to pay the dividends sheds even more light on the matter.

available to foreigners and to protect land in distress but not available to foreigners; a trust bank, however, of an entirely different nature [than Hirsch's].) What steps should be taken to influence developments in this direction? And there are many other questions that cannot be answered at this point. Since share capital provides the most convenient form of foreign ownership, one might welcome the shop-council law as an antidote to the cultural losses occasioned by foreign control if only the socialistic instruction directed at the citizenry focused more on economy.

IV. Inflation and the Exchange Rate

The preceding section shed light on the nature of the exchange rate by noting the impossibility of paying for foreign goods in some way other than with domestic products (goods and services) or by transferring ownership of domestic real estate abroad. In between there is provisional payment in the form of loans and credit. The exchange rate is the immediate and public expression of a country's situation in this regard. This is true in the sense that the change in the rate from one point to another as well as the respective absolute rate indicate the direction of current developments. The huge difference between the private (in the business, civil sense) settlement of international debt and the overall balance of trade cannot be emphasized strongly and often enough. To settle his foreign debts (or recover his foreign receivables), the individual can employ every conceivable means that achieves his goal and the debt still remains unpaid from an economy-wide point of view. A debtor, for example, can issue a bill of acceptance to a foreign creditor. He pays this bill on demand and discharges his debt. The domestic bank that collects the bill, however, is from then on the debtor to the foreign country instead of the original debtor. And if this bank then purchases a check or remittance made out to the foreign creditor on the money market or from a foreign exchange dealer, it discharges its foreign debt as well. With regard to the foreign exchange dealer, there are two possibilities: either the foreign currency he sells derives from goods exported abroad (which in the end means goods paid with goods), or his foreign business correspondent, in whose favor he has drawn the check or remittance, extends the amount on credit. In the overall economic context this means that the foreign business correspondent now replaces the original creditor. Thus, the international debt persists.

Substituting the bill of acceptance with a government or private debenture only substitutes one domestic debtor for another. The international debt situation remains unchanged. The sum in question, however, is withdrawn from the currency market and its pressure on the exchange rate is relieved. This advantageous effect lingers as long as the amount remains as a fixed investment. When the debenture has to be repaid pressure is exerted on the exchange rate once again; in the meantime, moreover, there is the pressure of having continuously to pay interest. The effect is not much different when the foreign country acquires domestic property in payment of the debt.

The amounts due to foreign creditors exert no pressure on the exchange rate as long as the money remains within the country. But even in that case the profit accrues to the foreign country and has to be "made available in the form of foreign currency," that is, to pay for it we have to part with goods, services, or more domestic real estate. The war reparations demands are made of us in exchange for nothing and thus have the same effect as debt for imported goods. The billions of marks floating abroad should be understood in the following context: once they cross the border they create a reciprocal debt relationship. The sender of mark notes abroad becomes a creditor vis-à-vis the other country, and his debtor, the foreigner who receives the notes, becomes a creditor of the Reichsbank. These two relationships, of course, offset one another as long as no goods are imported for the quantity of marks sent abroad. The importation of goods, however, results in a situation no better or worse than if no mark notes were sent abroad. The entire national economy is in debt for the value of these goods but not also in debt for the notes.

The disturbing thing about this floating quantity of marks is its outward form as money, which makes it seem to be in the wrong hands when it ought to be flowing back into the country in the form of German bank deposits. This return inflow is, of course, impossible since Germany continues to import an ever greater volume of foreign goods. A plan has been contemplated whereby German industry associations would float huge loans abroad. The loans would take the floating mark notes off the money markets and, ultimately, provide capital for the German economy. If one substitutes the term "working capital" for "capital" here, one understands that the plan is a matter of form over substance. In the end, it is a question of converting short-term foreign claims for working capital (raw materials) already supplied, which heretofore have been covered with Reichsbank notes, into long-term industrial bonds. Industry's additional working capital requirements are not met in this way but remain unfulfilled. Once again foreign countries would become owners of German property and holders of German bonds. Of course implementation of the plan would have a favorable effect on the exchange rate, but not because the notes would be taken off the market, rather because the unpaid claims against Germany would be taken off the market.

If one considers the future of the exchange rate in light of the German balance of payments (including the effects of the reparations demands placed on us), one thing is certain: the exchange rate will be under continuous pressure from abroad because of our overwhelming demand for foreign goods of all kinds. We are dependent on foreign capital to replenish our stocks of inventories and to pay reparations. Thus, foreign capital provides in part the goods we import and in part our reparations payments. Obviously, it can only make up the lesser part of the burden. We have to bear the brunt ourselves by increasing our labor output as compared to 1914 and by restricting our needs even as compared to our [reduced] standards today. To reduce the pressure on the exchange rate, we must make provisions for the earliest possible and greatest possible assumption of control by foreign interests. We must do so by achieving peace domestically and structuring such foreign control in the least disagreeable manner possible. What actions foreign interests will take once we achieve domestic tranquility is best exemplified by the Dutch company Protectrix (*Kölnische Zeitung*, no. 343). The same is true if the exchange rate is to be improved. Since the exchange rate serves as the communicating tube between domestic price formation and world market prices, every improvement in the exchange rate means that, correspondingly, a larger number of small and medium-sized businesses (on which Germany's well-being heavily depends) can survive. Further deterioration, on the other hand, will eliminate more and more of these businesses.

To improve the exchange rate, that is, to increase the value of the mark abroad, we must not only concentrate on substantive strategies such as structuring foreign control to our advantage (and obviously by increasing exports), but on formal strategies as well, such as ingenious technical manipulations of the all-powerful exchange rate. Foreign exchange loans are in between substance and form. It is not entirely a question of turning black facts into white ones on the basis of form, rather it is a question of acting in opposition to the foreign exchange speculations of the entire world and carefully cultivating the exchange rate (if not supporting it outright with counterspeculation) and thus gaining ground inch by inch. It would, however, have to be a very flexible arrangement free from the strict forms and friction of the war economy line of thinking. And we ought to gladly pay whatever price we must in this regard.

I conclude my observations at this point. An enormous increase in labor output, vast restrictions on all our daily needs (as long as price controls exist neither factor can be given sufficient free play), foreign credits at usurious interest rates, and foreign ownership of German property on a grand scale are our future and our salvation.   Neither communism nor socialism can ease our lot. They can only worsen it. Every war lost has produced the same effect, only the forms change. We can even expect intelligent and handsome people to be dragged away into slavery. What did our enemies say about bleeding us dry when we were admonished to hold out to the end?

4. Accounting Problems[*]

Erwin Geldmacher

I.

The terrible legacy of the war, the constantly falling purchasing power of the Reichsmark, shrouds German business enterprises like Nessus's tunic. Amidst the ever thicker confetti shower of paper money, many simply do not see that businesses are bleeding to death. Workers and employers, "proletarians" and "capitalists" are locked in grim conflict. Their very life source, the enterprise, is running dry.

"But substantial profits have been made from the war!" If they ever existed, they are long since gone. "But there are still extensive reserve funds!" Just like leaky, almost empty barrels with deceptive labels. "Balance sheets published nowadays still present the same picture as they did in 1913 and 1914!" An alarming insight: assets and equities (capital!) would have to have inflated five times or more if they were to match their earlier counterparts. "Annual profits are growing. Many balance sheets indicate as much!" Mere tricks with figures; a sign of flourishing, galloping consumption. Profit-and-loss accounting has been sabotaged; it is misleading in this day and age!

"Prove it!" I shall offer a schematically simple example that will allow things to be seen as they are through the money haze.

On 1 January 1919 a piano dealer had ten pianos that cost 1,000 M. each, including all expenses. He adds a mark-up of 10% on cost. He ekes out a scanty living from this profit. He has no credit and extends no credit. Assume four accounting periods. The cost of a similar piano rises during these four periods from 1,000 M. to 2,000 M., then to 5,000 M., and finally to 10,000 M. This represents a tenfold increase for the year.

This example is very basic; in reality, buying, selling, and cost increases tend not to go in fits and starts as they do here. But this example is not a lame one. It is meant to be very basic. A tenfold increase in prices may seem quite substantial; it certainly is not unusual. Of course prices will not have risen so fast before, but the effect of a rapid rise

[*]   *Industrie- und Handelszeitung*, October 1920, pp. 364, 378, 384, 392, 398, and 406.

in prices is to be made obvious here so that the ramifications can be seen all the more clearly. Have not great numbers of businessmen been lamenting - especially since November 1919 - that the money they receive from sale of their goods and products is often far less than what they have to pay for immediate replacement of the goods sold? Of course matters are much more complicated in commerce and industry, but the situation is not fundamentally different from our example. Only in banks, whose "goods" are money and monetary equivalents, have things developed somewhat differently: giants have turned into dwarves.[1] They have, however, undergone this transformation without experiencing any life-threatening functional disorders; even as Lilliputians they folic about quite merrily. They will not die of consumption like other businesses, but from a stroke; not from a diseased monetary system, but from its total breakdown.

In the case of the piano dealer the course of his business could be shown as follows:

Time	Number of Pianos	Cost	Revenue
1st quarter	10 Pianos at 1,000 M.	10,000 M.	11,000 M.
2nd quarter	5 Pianos at 2,000 M.	10,000 M.	11,000 M.
3rd quarter	2 Pianos at 5,000 M.	10,000 M.	11,000 M.
4th quarter	1 Piano at 10,000 M.	10,000 M.	Not sold

Opening Balance Sheet 1 January 1919		Closing Balance Sheet 31 December 1919	
10 Pianos: 10,000 M.	Capital: 10,000 M.	1 Piano: 10,000 M. Cash or Private Account: 3,000 M.	Capital: 10,000 M. Profit: 3,000 M.
		13,000 M.	13,000 M.

The dealer has calculated as he did in the good old days: cost + 10%. (The 10% is of no concern here; what is important is the price formation process and its reliance on historical cost.) The piano dealer's profit-and-loss account indicates that he has made a

1   At the beginning of December 1919 the Dutch calculated per the Amsterdam conversion rate of 6 gilder = 100 M. that the eight largest Dutch banks had a collective capital of 9 billion M. compared to that of only 1.9 billion M. held by the eight largest German banks. In light of the weaker exchange rate, the power ratio is even more unfavorable for the once so proud German banks today.

"profit" of 3,000 M. before taxes. He started the year with ten pianos and now he has one left! When he has sold that one, he cannot acquire any more new pianos and will have to close his business.

Had the dealer not sold his ten pianos, he would have had neither profit nor income; but he would own ten pianos of the same quality, of which he now has one. In addition, there is the sobering thought that if he sold them now, he would realize over 100,000 M. But then he would have been a profiteer and not an honorable merchant. And because he is honorable, he only has one piano left and can no longer be a dealer. Perhaps his next step is to apply for unemployment benefits. Is it not absurd that the dealer, who initially had ten pianos, who sold these ten plus seven more, and who still has one left, should nevertheless make a "profit" of 3,000 M., which he then has to report to the tax authorities as income. And to think that he does so in accordance with proper bookkeeping procedures that are irreproachable in both the business and legal sense. Actually, however, his accounting is wrong!

II.

In the preceding section we questioned the legitimacy of the dealer's profit-and-loss calculation. We now turn our attention to his costing practices. Should not the dealer have said to himself: whatever the circumstances I must set selling price so that I maintain my base stock as to both quantity and quality, so that I maintain the vitality of my business despite all the perils of monetary deterioration? Perhaps he thinks this way - economically. If so, he would arrive at the following principle: I must base my cost calculations not on outdated historical costs, but on replacement costs valid at the time of sale. In doing so, he can even rely on an eminent researcher in the field of business economics. Professor Dr. Schmalenbach of the University of Cologne wrote in his 1908 article "Theory of Production Costs " (*Zeitschr. f. handelswiss. Forsch.,* vol. 3, p. 50):

> Practice generally conforms to the theory that production costs, that is, when production costs are to serve price formation purposes, must be based on costs actually paid. I would like to counter this view with the theory that inventory values in particular should move with fluctuating prices and that an enterprise's accounts should be debited with prices that prevail when asset consumption occurs.

To be sure, Schmalenbach wrote this during peacetime, when the currency was in a healthy state and when a businessman could operate his business according to sound economic principles and not come into conflict with moral standards or the law. But we are still dragging around with us such a heavy ballast of outmoded views and methods that we ought for once to apply a fundamentally correct economic principle regardless, without a sidelong glance to the left or the right. In the example above, the piano dealer, had his instinct for self preservation made him aware of this principle, would have had the following business experience in 1919:

Time	Number of Pianos	Cost	Revenue
1st quarter	10 pianos, at 1,000 M.	10,000 M.	22,000 M.
2nd quarter	10 pianos, at 2,000 M.	20,000 M.	55,000 M.
3rd quarter	10 pianos, at 5,000 M.	50,000 M.	110,000 M.
4th quarter	10 pianos, at 10,000 M.	100,000 M.	Unsold

Opening Balance Sheet 1 January 1919		Closing Balance Sheet 31 December 1919	

10 Pianos:
    10,000 M.
	Capital:
	    10,000 M.
		1 Piano:
		    100,000 M.
		Cash or Private
		Account:
		    17,000 M.
			Capital:
			    10,000 M.
			
			Profit:
			    107,000 M.

		117,000 M.	117,000 M.

This display of figures is grotesque. Consider the results first through the eyes of tradition, "as the law requires." According to standard bookkeeping the dealer has a net profit of 107,000 M.; any expert bookkeeper would confirm this. The dealer is a profitmonger of the worst sort, and anyone who thinks "along legal lines" must condemn him. The dealer will not enjoy "his robbery": if he is not seized by the courts for extortion, the tax authorities will. One hundred and seven thousand marks net profit is a lucrative tax object, especially at the close of 1919. To be sure, the dealer has already used much of the 17,000 M. cash for himself and his family in the taxable year 1919, but he still has ten pianos at 10,000 M. each which can be seized and auctioned - what is law is law. Under the law, moreover, the extortionist now belongs in jail.

Now put aside the traditional viewpoint and consider the matter from an objective, economic point of view. The dealer simply wanted to maintain his business. In doing so, he looked at the substance without unduly concerning himself with the numbers. At the end of the year he still had ten pianos of the same kind he had at the beginning of the year. Effectively, he had maintained his business on the same scale. Furthermore, he had realized 17,000 M. cash to provide for his family and himself. Naturally he considers this 17,000 M. as profit, as remuneration for having sold 30 pianos during the year, for he already had the stock of ten pianos at the beginning of the year. The net profit of 17,000 M. cash does not seem too high to him because it is no mean task to sell 30 pianos these days. If he pays tax from the 17,000 M., he will really feel it in today's environment.

But now this *homo economicus* has to believe that a wrongful tax law is depriving him of the very resources he needs to run his business, robbing him of the very basis of his existance; that the excess-profits law is doing him terrible injustice and indeed holds him personally responsible for "the contrariness of things," for the high prices that have resulted from scarcity and inflation. And only him and those like him, that is, self-employed businessmen. For when economically dependent persons - laborers, employees, and bureaucrats - sell their services at a figure several times higher than it used to be, no one would dare say that that was profiteering. For workers and salaried employees must have their living wage regardless of inflation. Otherwise they will starve. Our piano dealer acted on the same impulse; he does not want his business to starve, and its "living wage" consists of ten pianos. And only if he bases selling prices on respective replacement costs can he maintain the viability of his enterprise. What is more, he can only assure himself an income if he adds an appropriate mark-up on cost determined in this way. Operationally, this is the only policy that eliminates the mortal danger accelerating inflation holds for a business enterprise.

Yet the profit-and-loss account of the dealer in the above example shows a correctly calculated profit of 107,000 M. And if the dealer wants to quarrel with the tax authorities and the excess-profits law, he must surely despair of his original calculations, that is, of traditional commercial bookkeeping. These days his own profit-and-loss account, this marvel of precise accounting, is making a fool of him. It provides the documentary evidence of his "guilt." He will have no trouble relating the profit-and-loss account to the rule of thumb that "the law perpetuates itself like a perennial disease."

III.

Schmalenbach terms profit "the measure of the operating efficiency" of an enterprise; profit is "the surplus of an enterprise's output over its outlays!" Further, "accounting should be regarded as a means of calculating profit."

Accounting *was* to be regarded as a means of calculating profit. Without doubt commercial bookkeeping fulfilled this fundamental purpose in the pre-war years, that is, it served as a means of accurately calculating profit. In the pre-war years the dealer might have accounted as follows:

Time	Number of Pianos			Cost	Revenue
1st quarter	10 pianos at	1,000 M.		10,000 M.	11,000 M.
2nd quarter	10 pianos at	1,050 M.		10,500 M.	11,550 M.
3rd quarter	10 pianos at	950 M.		9,500 M.	10,450 M.
4th quarter	10 pianos at	1,000 M.		1,000 M.	Unsold

Opening Balance Sheet 1 January 1913		Closing Balance Sheet 31 December 1913	
10 pianos: 　　10,000 M.	Capital: 　　10,000 M.	1 piano: 　　　　10,000 M. Cash or Private Account: 　　　　3,000 M.	Capital: 　　10,000 M. Profit: 　　3,000 M.
		13,000 M.	13,000 M.

Thus, in pre-war times the dealer would have had a viable business and adequate remuneration for his work. What is more, the profit figure would have been a true measure of the operating efficiency of his business. Whether the businessman costed on the basis of historical cost or replacement cost made very little difference to the survival of the business. Given the comparatively insignificant changes in prices at the time, he could use the latter basis and never be accused of profiteering. Most importantly: the price actually obtained did not result from the costing practices of individual enterprises, but from free-market, often global competition. The organized efforts of businessmen made huge inventories available; business and trade ensured that such abundance was available everywhere; demand was never so starved as it is today. Price formation was flexibly anchored between supply and demand, and a clinging money gown showed things as they really were. The Reichsmark was an almost ideal measure of outlay and output and their result: profit or loss.

Nowadays a state of anarchy reigns in the economy. If inventories are exhausted and hard work can no longer replenish them, demand, voracious as it is, must surely grow immeasurably. And prices along with it. Now it whirls about in a harlequin's costume of an evanescent currency; now it leaps like a Cossack. But Ash Wednesday is coming. The truth holds: who does not work, shall not eat. Soon it will be even worse: who cannot work, cannot eat either, for the workplaces of millions of Germans - business enterprises-are wasting away.

It would be curious if commercial profit-and-loss accounting, which is so closely tied to the monetary system, had not suffered internal damage as the Reichsmark deteriorated. A comparison of the course of trade in pre-war times with the two accounting schemata from the present reveals the devastating influence of inflation and monetary disintegration on business management and income determination.

Accounting during the war according to old costing principles resulted in a "profit" of 3,000 M., but the business perished in the process. Accounting for the same transactions according to new economic costing principles (which *today* seem harmful to the economy and *today* are morally reprehensible, but which from a business economics point of view are absolutely correct) resulted in a "profit" of 107,000 M. In this case, the business liquidated because of taxes and penalties. No business-economics-minded person would say that in either case the profit figure, "the measure of operating efficiency," (which was determined by standard bookkeeping procedures) indicates the "surplus of output over outlay." For in the first case the business "has consumed more materials and labor than it has achieved in output." The profit figure of 3,000 M. is an absurd farce. In the second case, it is true that the enterprise conducted its business unjustly and immorally and realized a surplus, but the profit figure of 107,000 M. does not correspond to the actual surplus of output over outlay. It is greatly exaggerated.

It must be sharply emphasized that the implied condition for the vehicle of income determination, commercial bookkeeping, to function properly is a relatively stable currency and price trend! Naturally there was no absolute stability before the war; everything to do with economics is relative. But when we compare the insignificant fluctuations in the guilder rate before the war with the huge and erratic increases since the war, we have a fair comparative picture of the price trends in both these periods.

Regarding the first wartime accounting schema, I might add that there is no question that a business is operating inefficiently when it begins to waste away, when there are fewer and fewer real values behind the balance sheet figures, when the balance sheet items more nearly resemble poorly produced cardboard tubes than power-filled accumulators. Many balance sheets published by large companies these days give this lamentable picture.

Of more interest to us is the second wartime accounting schema which provides an antidote to this widespread misuse and the relatively ample inventories of many businesses indicate that a good number of them have developed a taste for modern costing methods. The example of the 107,000 M. profit figure indicates as much. One can be quite sure that with any vigorous activity on the part of the tax authorities taxes on "gainful employment," the new Reich income tax, the corporate income tax, the war-profits and capital appreciation taxes, the new sales tax, and the Reich emergency tax will far exceed any advance estimate. And many a businessman will sit and sweat behind his profit-and-loss figures. It will dawn on him that behind these inflated profit figures are the liquidation results, measured in paper marks, of his old stock of operational assets.

IV.

It can be shown mathematically that in times of erratic price increases and a depreciating currency traditional commercial income determination no longer applies.

The profit-and-loss account itself is based on subtraction like any other account; the row of figures on the weaker side is deducted from the figures on the stronger side. Use of the account presupposes two things: one can only combine increases and decreases expressed in exactly the same terms. Thus, all increases and decreases must be measured by a uniform standard (e.g., kg or m). The uniform measure, whose total annual increases and decreases are combined in the profit-and-loss account, represents the businessman's absolute authority over the operational assets shown on the debit side and equals the amount termed "capital" in bookkeeping. The annual increases in capital are termed "revenues" (output), while the annual decreases are referred to as "expenses"; the result, or difference, is profit or loss. The common measure for revenues and expenses is money, in our case the Reichsmark. These days, however, we can compare the Reichsmark to a folding rule, which becomes shorter and shorter, but which in the various stages of collapse continues to be used as a 1 m rule, so that a silk ribbon measuring 1 m (and whose length remains unchanged) would be measured as 2, 5, 9, then 12 m successively. It would be mathematical nonsense if one added or subtracted the meter amounts at the various stages.

But this mathematical nonsense is what is happening in the profit-and-loss account today.[2] Expense items are measured in Reichsmarks of a different character than those of revenue items. The expense side always shows mark amounts of a higher real value than those shown on the revenue side. This is true because all expenses precede revenues and in the interval the Reichsmark loses additional purchasing power. On the expense side there are even gold-mark amounts from pre-war days, namely the annual depreciation quotas that began before the war. On the revenue side there are only paper-mark amounts from the current inflationary year. In addition, each successive mark amount has less purchasing power than its predecessor. Further, value developments for expense items cease once the items are entered (or, more precisely, once they are consumed), whereas value developments for revenue items continue. This means that during periods of continuing inflation revenue amounts lose value parallel to the ongoing loss in value of related assets (such as cash, bank credits, accounts receivable). In sum, all this means that the items on both sides of the profit-and-loss account are measured in marks of varying value and, above all, that total expenses are recorded in better marks than total revenues.

In mathematical terms, this means that two measures from different scales are being combined in one balance! The mark is simply no longer a common and faithful measure for expenses and revenues (output). Just as one cannot subtract Nordic kroner from

---

[2]   The insignificant changes in the purchasing power of the mark prior to the war, which may be compared to the fluctuations in the length of a platinum bar at different temperatures, meant that profit-and-loss calculations at the time were for all practical purposes not incorrect.

Germano-Austrian kroner and obtain a useful difference, one cannot subtract higher-value marks from lower-value marks in the profit-and-loss account and conclude that the balance represents profit. But this is exactly what commercial profit-and-loss accounting does today. And it is on this kind of "profit" that the tax authorities base their income tax assessments, etc.

Of course the comparison of the mark with the folding rule is inappropriate in that one can determine precisely the changes in the length of a rule by the unchanging length of the object measured. Using the mark as a measure of value, however, one cannot distinguish arithmetically to what extent inflation has contributed to the increase in the price of the object measured and to what extent a change in the value of the object itself. But this distinction is not necessary for the present argument. It is enough to demonstrate that the huge ongoing loss in the purchasing power of money, which is a result of the inflationary factors enumerated above, has made the figures in the profit-and-loss account a mathematical monstrosity.

If the dealer in the example had not sold his pianos, if he had not acted as a salesman, his base stock would not have assumed its exorbitant paper-mark value. It is a peculiarity of merchandise inventory that it is forced through the money filter again and again, and that today, as the money filter changes from day to day, the degree of its dilution is determined by the most recent filter. In other words, everything depends on brisk activity in industry and commerce. Yet today this same activity is punished and crippled by a tax policy that does not adequately take into account the revolutionary change in the monetary system nor in the related profit account. The risk becomes greater and greater that goods held back and hoarded, not just merchandise inventory, will be seen by the tax authorities through the magnifying glass of the most recent monetary situation. Nowadays *homo economicus* suffers losses if he remains true to his nature.

One may object that the course of business depicted in the first two accounting schemata is too gloomy. Certainly they represent extreme cases. Actually, accounting today lies between the two extremes, which means that businesses are bleeding to death slowly. In regard to his pricing policy, many a businessman finds himself between Scylla and Charibdis: he cannot simply let his business die and he does not want to come into conflict with the excess-profits law or official price regulations. From a purely business economics point of view, the businessman should only use replacement costs for costing purposes. In many lines of business there is no small risk attached to this. As a consequence, there is a lack of economically rational behaviour. Naturally, it is often the case that when turnover is fast the large mark-ups on cost (among other things, the great differences in prices one often finds in the same shop for the same goods, a situation that often favors the consumer, proves that many businessmen have not abandoned this uneconomic principle) yield such high proceeds that they suffice to make the most essential additional acquisitions. These businesses then suffer only from incorrect profit calculations and their consequence, excessive taxes. But most businesses are actually destitute; behind all the accounting figures there is no more vitality. This applies particularly to businesses that rely on overseas markets, e.g., the entire textile industry. The huge infusions of capital that almost all joint-stock companies have experienced (from November 1919 to January 1920 ca. 2½ billion marks) barely suffice to make up for the debilitation they have already suffered. If prices continue to rise at such a headlong rate, these infusions of capital will be of no use at all.

V.

The deterioration of profit-and-loss accounting has not occurred evenly in all lines of business. Enterprises engaged in primary production have suffered less than manufacturing and retails enterprises. In the case of enterprises whose operation depends purely on labor, such as a mill, traditional income determination still provides fairly accurate results. Even more businesses ought to become labor-oriented enterprises. Foreign countries are preparing to devour the mouth-watering spoils. The threat of slave labor is growing.

The business economics antidote - price formation on the basis of replacement cost - has the economy-wide effect of driving prices higher, just like wage increases. It has also been branded as profiteering. Corruption is turning into a plague which threatens to contaminate everything. The temptation to engage in "double-entry" bookkeeping in the negative sense of the word is growing. Profiteering of the sort that keeps no books and evades taxation is gaining ground. The waste of funds held back to avoid taxation is increasing, which, in turn, aggravates their scarcity. Deliberate falsification of balance sheets is also increasing: large stocks of inventories are not accounted for. Since goods are taking the place of money as a store of value, they are withheld. People are "dealing" in the economic boom. This is a capitalist's strike which is sure to succeed. The larger businesses start things off (it is not so noticeable with them) and the retailers follow. Barter is thriving. Barter allows exchanges to be measured in terms of the old value of money and to avoid taxes assessed on today's values.

In sum, the most important consequences of a profit-and-loss calculation that has become economically incorrect are as follows. There may be:

·   incorrect business management;

·   incorrect measurement of crucial outlays, for example, excessive distributions of net profit, for example, depreciation, dividends;

·   intentional falsification of balance sheets;

·   intensification of the social antagonism between wage and salary earners and company management; and

·   ruinous taxation of a business's essential stock of productive assets.

What can be done to overcome the harm caused by today's incorrect profit calculation?

Profit is a phenomenon of economy-wide interest. Society as a whole depends on business enterprises to use no more materials and labor than they achieve in output. Society must insist that all economic activity be carried out profitably. Just as it is a matter of concern for the general public that the businessman pursue his vocation with the public interest at heart, it is also a matter of concern for the general public that the businessman not incorrectly calculate the measure of his operating efficiency - his profit.

These truly meaningful words of Schmalenbach were directed primarily against "the diabolical and socially noxious idea held by many businessmen" that "correct calculation of enterprise profit is a matter for the businessman alone." Those called upon to contribute in a major way to the preservation and reconstruction of the German economy as well as to tax legislation need to be especially conscious of these words today. Any businesses that are economically viable should be saved. The days of well-worn and familiar ways are over; new ways must be found. Commercial law is nothing but an abstraction from commercial life and must change when commercial life itself has changed. The law must follow the economy, not oppose it. It is not a matter of protecting "capitalistic" interests; rather, there is an eminently important social need to ensure that the very life of the jobs of most Germans is not further drained and ultimately spent as a result of incorrect income calculations and the incorrect taxes and dividend distributions based on them.

Assume that Germany's legislative bodies decided all at once, before it was too late, to protect the vital fixed assets and inventories of business enterprises (perhaps by partially freezing owners' rights of disposal) from further impairment due to taxation and profit distributions as well as from threat of dismantlement to satisfy foreign interests. How might the plan be structured? What steps might be taken to correct today's economically incorrect income calculations?

The base stock of assets subject to legal protection would, of course, vary from business to business. Committees of experts, preferably agents of the accounting offices mentioned below, would have to assess in detail what particular assets needed protection. The result, legally speaking, would be a stock of assets which would not be taxable regardless of their current value in marks. These committees could also establish norms for the depreciation and replacements of individual enterprises. As a matter of principle, the establishment of norms for an enterprise's stock of essential fixed assets and inventories is envisioned as a summary statement of kind and quantity based on holdings as of, say, 31 December 1918. Of course only the most essential assets could be included. In this way, a prototypical cross section of the most important asset groups would be created. An accounting office, to which appointed trustees and honorary representatives of chambers of commerce might belong, would examine annually companies' customary balance sheets and profit-and-loss accounts, which the companies themselves would have to submit in uncorrected form. The accounting office would perform the examination according to the particular enterprise's basic plan and make any necessary adjustment on the liabilities side of the balance sheet.

The second wartime accounting schema can serve as a simple example for the technical side of this proposal. The schema showed an economically nonsensical profit figure of 107,000 M. The figure requires correction. The piano dealer had ten pianos in stock, which were worth 10,000 M. at the beginning of the year and 100,000 M. at the end of the year. Thus, the 107,000 M. profit figure contains 90,000 M. capital and 17,000 M. profit. The correction in this case would be made by means of the following entry:

Dr. profit and loss   90,000

       Cr.   capital (in the case of joint-stock
            companies credit the common stock
            reserve account) for revaluation of
            enterprise base assets   90,000

This entry would correct the profit-and-loss account provided current principles of economics remained in effect, and the keystone of commercial accounting - profit - would once again constitute the measure of enterprise operating efficiency.

V.

(Conclusion)

In terms of tax law this proposal means that the businessman's base assets are revalued as a result of their continuing use in operations. The businessman can earn nothing on his base stock, just as a private person can earn nothing on his old household goods, even if prices for such goods have risen ten times since their acquisition. The above proposal entails exactly the same protection for assets essential to the operation of a business as the current tax law offers for household goods up to 20,000 M., although there can be no question of a universal mark limit. Business enterprises are far too diverse. From a business point of view, the 90,000 M. correction in the example represents a portion of original enterprise capital; from a legal point of view, it represents a portion of a prior stock of assets which has remained physically intact, but which is now seen through the magnifying glass of today's currency. Should the proposed law be approved for business enterprises, it would mean in the case of the example above: the 90,000 M. adjustment does not constitute capital gain, the war tax on capital gains does not apply. The adjustment is even less an object for the assessment of income taxes, excess-profits taxes, and corporate taxes. These taxes relate only to the remaining 17,000 M., which represent a real, economic profit.

The advantage of the proposal is that businessmen can continue to account as they always have and prepare balance sheets and profit-and-loss accounts. Given the lack of theoretical training on the part of the great majority of businessmen (who are at a complete loss as to the reasons for the breakdown of their income calculations), the advantage is great indeed: the cogwheels can turn in the same old grooves. In any event, the correction only requires a single entry. The one entry would pull the rug from under those who feel the urge to doctor the balance sheet - and the urge must be particularly strong these days. *Balance sheets would remain intelligible in every instance.* If, for example, at the end of the second fiscal year of the war only 8 pianos were on hand, but available cash was 20,000 M. greater, the correcting entry would be the same; for the enterprise protection plan was based on a base stock of not 8, but 10 pianos. Whether the other 2 pianos are in stock or on order makes no difference as far as the correcting entry in concerned. It only represents an adjustment between capital and appreciation (profit). The asset side of the balance sheet would remain unchanged - a picture for all who read balance sheets: businessmen, shareholders, banks, creditors in general, auditors, and revenue officers. With this technique in use, the continuity of balance sheets (that is, their concatenation), which has been broken by rising prices and the appalling deterioration of the currency, would find outward expression in only one point, the capital account. If, on the other hand, one were to undertake to correct each asset account individually, one would obtain such bizarre balance sheets (the enormity of price increases would not be compatible with the historical amounts in the base asset accounts) that only a few experts could understand them.

The intelligibility of balance sheets is infinitely more important today than in normal times. The profit-and-loss account no longer occupies the center of our attention. The balance sheet does! There are two reasons for this. First, as I have sought to demonstrate here, in almost every business today's profit-and-loss account is clouded, distorted, misleading. Even in a purely mathematical sense it is a jigsaw puzzle. Above all, however, the motivation for economic endeavor has been significantly dampened. In these stormy times when German businesses are struggling for their very existence, they have had to adopt more modest goals. Today it is primarily a matter of maintaining the status quo. Any profit realized over and above that goal is in the eyes of most businesses a stroke of luck. The touchstone of an enterprise's operating efficiency, accordingly, is not so much its profit-or-loss calculation, which is supposed to evidence efficiency in a profit figure but which has degenerated and become misleading. Rather, it is the balance sheet, which makes possible a judgment as to whether and to what extent a business has been successfully maintained. For this reason it is imperative that balance sheets be kept readable, even if this means placing businesses under the protection of the law and requiring correcting entries. There has been an analogous shift in the valuation of share capital, for the boom market stems not primarily from earnings expectations as it once did but from the desire to preserve capital.

The proposal to draw a legal wall around imperiled businesses means, of course, limiting the autonomy of business owners, but it will put an end to all the petty secrecy. This action alone will save business enterprises. I will not discuss here how widely the circle should be drawn, whether or not enterprise subordination to accounting offices should be compulsory or voluntary, or whether a mixed system would be appropriate. One should keep in mind that law and economics are widely divergent today and that we are witnessing unbridled price fluctuations (wherein lies the cause of our accounting problems). Attempts by businesses to help themselves have failed; the state must act. It is important in these times when all values are in a state of flux that each and every enterprise remain viable, that each enterprise's operational efficiency be determined beyond doubt, that taxation not destroy the economy. If profit is what one wants, the way via recapitalization over and above one's stock of base assets remains open.

Above all, however, it is the responsibility of legislators more than ever to concern themselves with the maintenance of the material basis of German enterprises. Achieving this goal is vital, affecting as it does 60 million hungry people. Consider the cause of our economic woes. Thinking in terms of the balance sheet will clarify matters: when, as a matter of financial exigency, the number of banknotes (Germany's liabilities) that in normal times corresponds to a fixed complex of goods (Germany's assets) is doubled, prices double as well. If the supply of goods simultaneously diminishes by one half, prices will double yet again. (This is correct in principle. In the real world all kinds of frictions prevent such an exact mathematical result.) In effect, prices quadruple. If a man has held on to a certain quantity of goods, the tax authorities will then come along and declare that three fourths of his goods are profit, income, appreciation! This is how enormous profits are generated these days - on paper. Meanwhile the economy bleeds to death from a thousand wounds. There is a remarkably uneconomic bent to the conceptual basis of our tax law. One simply compares old mark figures with current mark figures and taxes the difference. One need only keep the paper money presses rolling to increase all "income" and thus to increase all taxes. The poorer we become in concrete assets, the richer we are in figures. This noose of figures cannot continue to strangle the physical organism of our enterprises. The Russian example is frightening enough; our economic machinery, however, is much more complex, and its destruction much more perilous than in agrarian Russia. Do we really want to let our companies continue to waste away? Those who can see through the haze of the money sphinx have, to date, only seen this downward sloping path.

The proposal I have offered here is only a preventative, not a cure. Healing all our economic ills would require a stabilized monetary system, and, above all else, the hardest work by everyone while living the simplest of life-styles.

Traditional commercial income calculation will provide a true picture of the profitability of companies again only when equable price developments are achieved. Such equability only depends on prices stabilizing at some given level. It does not have to be the previous price level. Stabilization, however, does not appear possible in the foreseeable future. All value relationships have fallen into a truly Babylonian confusion following the breakdown of the monetary system and the separation of the German economy from the organism of the world economy. In the final analysis it is this easing of previously fixed value relationships among assets that is so destructive of our balance sheets. The economist used to see the picture of an economic organism pulsating with robust life - an integrated whole - in his balance sheets. Today he sees himself pushed more and more into the position of a legal observer asking much as a trustee in bankruptcy: what's behind these - assets? Treating these questions from the standpoint of proprietary law pushes the business economics point of view too far into the background. To use a drastic analogy: when a farmer's milk cow has become anemic and unproductive, the butcher appraises her by dead weight.   Certainly higher taxes are inevitable when the money presses are finally stilled and the German monetary system is restored.   But the consuls may wish to make sure that all the milk cows are not slaughtered.

5. Depreciation or Replacement?*

G. Schlesinger
Charlottenburg

"How is it possible," a shop council member asked me in the spring of 1920, "that our firm's most recent profit-and-loss account contains several hundred thousand marks of depreciation expense when its entire stock of equipment has been fully depreciated for years? And why are the machinery accounts charged with such large amounts when additions were only minor?"

A difficult question indeed. In fact, it is the most pressing question an industrial manager faces today. How do I really account correctly? How do I allocate "profits" so that the enterprise survives the coming difficult times - so that it does not have to close its doors and dismiss its workers for lack of cash? So that my conscience as a conscientious businessman and bookkeeper remains clear? So that, finally, the tax authorities accept my tax returns as correct?

My dear Mr. Council Member, first of all we must come to an understanding of the term "depreciation"!

Because in practice depreciation is usually deducted as one large amount in arriving at net income, the concept of depreciation as savings set aside for the purpose of maintaining the enterprise through timely and appropriate replacement of the means of production has become obscured. People wrongly have become accustomed to viewing the amount of depreciation recognized as the option of the accountant, as a veiling of actual circumstances, as a diminution of undesirably high profits - profits one would prefer to hide from the public and thus from shareholders.

Concerning the possibility of reducing excessive profits, it should be explained that such "diminutional" depreciation immediately accrues to the enterprise, infusing it with new blood in the form of: machinery and tool enhancements; improvements in sanitary arrangements; better buildings; better lighting, heating, and ventilation; improved scientific research laboratories, etc.; all things that benefit the entire enterprise and all those employed in it. But even if these amounts are withheld from shareholders, i.e., from

---

*   *Werkstattstechnik*, vol. 14, 1 October 1920, 506-507.

"capitalists," for the common good of the enterprise, most struggles at general shareholders' meetings still can be attributed to shareholders seeking to prevent decreases in dividends due to depreciation they deem too large. For large amounts of depreciation mean small net profits. Shareholders and tax authorities, however, are only interested in large net profits. On this one point, at least, they agree.

"Depreciation," then, means: to transform concrete plant and equipment into liquid working capital, to put money back into the economy, and to keep the economy working at peak performance.

"Depreciation" means: to set aside savings in such amounts that all plant and equipment normally used in the enterprise may be continuously maintained or replaced from those savings.

For example, a semi-automatic machine is acquired today for 90,000 M. In approximately 5 years it will be so worn out and old that a new one will need to be acquired. After 5 years, accordingly, our savings account will have to contain 90,000 M. Thus, 90,000/5 = 18,000 M. will have to be depreciated (saved) annually. Proceeds from salvage value, however, may be deducted from that amount. At present, salvage value is estimated to be 10,000 M., so that the rate of depreciation becomes (90,000 − 10,000)/5 = 16,000 M. per year. Only if our savings account contains 80,000 M. in cash at the end of the 5 years is replacement of the worn-out semi-automatic machine possible. Only then can the enterprise continue to operate. And this simple argument holds for every item of plant and equipment - for buildings, transport equipment, furniture, stationery, etc.

Certainly the piece-rate operator of a rapidly deteriorating machine feels the wear and tear very directly as an impediment to earnings. Circumstances, however, are not always so straightforward and clear.

A patent that has protected an enterprise for years, for example, can be attacked and suddenly rendered worthless. As a result, the enterprise loses its monopoly position and enters free competition. It must update its perhaps obsolete, now unprotected plant, but has no savings from depreciation and must shut its doors. With the demise of the enterprise, its workers become destitute.

Therefore, Mr. Council Member, every enterprise family has a keen interest in depreciation that is correct and never too low.

And now for your other question? Is it possible to recognize tens of thousands in depreciation today on a machine that has been depreciated to one mark, and how does this necessity arise?

If you consider this matter exclusively from the standpoint of the traditional bookkeeping procedure that deducts 10 or 20 per cent of historical cost annually, there is no room for fresh hundreds of thousands in an account once it has been depreciated to one mark. But the old way of looking at things only holds under normal market and valuation conditions, i.e., conditions that depend on a stable currency; and our currency before the war was a gold currency subject to such minor fluctuations that for all practical purposes it could be regarded as a stable measure of value.

Measured by this standard, the value of an enterprise's entire plant remained the same yesterday, today, and tomorrow - ten years ago and ten years hence, just as the original measure of a meter has never changed.

This measure of value, the gold mark, was replaced by the paper mark during the war. Technically this means: the uniform measure of value changed. If one assumes that 10 gold marks are worth 150 paper marks, that means nothing more than that the same measure of value is being used today as previously except that each interval on the scale is fifteen times greater. The semi-automatic machine that cost 6,000 gold marks before the war costs 90,000 paper marks today (6 x 15). It is not in the least more valuable. We have just held a magnifying glass over it - a paper veil called inflation - and see things fifteenfold in the same way a drunk sees things double.

But that doesn't answer your question! To that end consider the following.

The semi-automatic machine that cost 6,000 marks in 1915 and that is no longer serviceable today has been depreciated 6,000 marks. This money is now in our enterprise savings account. And now this terrible war has simply transformed the 6,000 marks that are supposed to be "gold marks" into "paper marks." But a semi-automatic machine cannot be acquired today for 6,000 marks; we need 90,000 − 6,000 = 84,000 marks! A very large number of factory accountants did not even notice the apparently frictionless transition from a gold currency to a paper one. They thought that "Bookkeeping" would, as a matter of course, call such things to their attention on a timely basis; and today they make bookkeeping, which is a useful tool only in the skilled hands of experts, the scapegoat of their own foolishness. Even the sharpest and most useful tool wreaks havoc in the hands of the unskilled. Bookkeeping soon became rigidly conventional, and depreciation came to represent lifeless declines in value rather than the living concept of "constantly necessary replacement." Germany's 1919 "clearance sale" can be explained on the basis of this fundamental error. We sold without taking into account the necessity of replacement in terms of gold, and thus much too cheaply. Anyone who wants to replace plant and equipment on a timely basis and at full value must also retroactively replace superficially inflated values (gold values that have turned into paper through no fault of their own). For this reason one mark can swell to 84,000 marks in relation to a single machine in a fully depreciated machinery account with no particular event appearing to take place.

That answers your first question! You, Mr. Council Member, must in the interest of your fellow workers as well as your own see to it that the true meaning of depreciation, that of replacement at current values, supplants "depreciation in the tax sense." Otherwise all of you will be out of work when your worn-out and no longer replaceable enterprise shuts down. Anyone who has to replace plant (in the broadest sense) in terms of paper-marks needs enormous amounts of working capital, at present in multiples of fifteen at the very least, which one must either take from earned surplus or obtain by resorting to lines of credit with exorbitant interest rates.

But implementing the principles described here has another nasty catch that was alluded to above: the tax authorities have not yet recognized the concept of a "replacement account." For this reason the cautious manager is tempted to undervalue all sorts of accounts, such as inventory, rather than recognize large but correct amounts of depreciation aimed in all good faith at replacement - amounts that perhaps total more than the original mark values of the assets in question, but that create the reserves necessary to replace those assets. As a result, the balance sheet becomes distorted and discloses everything but the actual state of affairs. Rationalization of the tax laws, therefore, is one of the pressing issues of our time. Otherwise, as the saying goes, "Reason is becoming nonsense and charity evil, woe to posterity!"

In conclusion, I must call your attention to the sad fact that the value of our currency fluctuates sharply today. Thus, not only do we have a new standard of measure in use whose scale has been enlarged; unfortunately we also have a rubber standard of measure whose length expands and contracts daily. In terms of paper marks, a kilogram of brass cost 36 M. in early February, 26 M. in late February, and 20 M. today; a certain semi-automatic machine cost 42,000 M. in July 1919, 126,000 M. in early February 1920, and 90,000 M. today! How is one to know what value to use as a basis for depreciation as long as the mark is in such flux, as long as we cannot even guess whether wages, salaries, materials prices are going to go up or down? Would a cautious manager not prefer to reckon with a turn for the worse rather than a turn for the better and choose the highest value possible? That in doing so he disrupts the costing process is another important question whose treatment must be reserved for a future article.

6. Faulty Cost Accounting[*]

Gustav Kast,

Director, Frankfurt Trust and Audit, AG, Frankfurt am Main

Not a day goes by that one does not hear moaning and groaning about exorbitant industry prices, even in circles where one would expect a better grasp of the matter. The war turned a great deal on its head, including the simple principle that one cannot add apples and oranges. Indeed, the war tossed this principle out the window. For if one examines published balance sheets, one finds assets stemming from the pre-war period - assets stated in gold marks - simply added to post-war assets, which are stated in ever weaker paper marks, without a thought for the difference.

The same mistake is made in cost accounting. Here, too, people have not grasped the fact that the asset accounts on which depreciation is recognized for costing purposes consist of two entirely different values, gold mark and paper mark, and that these two values must be placed on an equal footing. The simplest way of accomplishing this is no doubt restatement in paper marks since the other cost elements - raw materials, wages, etc. - are expressed in paper marks, as are revenues from sales.

Assume that the relationship between gold marks and paper marks is 1:10 and that an enterprise still has machinery acquired before the war whose gold-mark cost was 100,000 M. and which has been depreciated at a rate of 10% per year. Cost charges would be calculated as follows:

10% of 100,000 gold marks or 1,000,000 paper marks	=	100,000 M.
paper-mark depreciation assuming no restatement (10% of 100,000 M.)	=	10,000 M.
amount by which work in process is undercharged annually		90,000 M.

One can arrive at no other outcome as long as one views cost calculation purely as a mathematical operation and fails to critically analyze the events and economic changes

---

that have a bearing on the process. In the example above, the cost accountants should be held accountable for the fact that one does not depreciate 10% per year and charge that amount to cost (which creates a reserve only in the amount of the numerical value of the machines at the end of their useful lives). Rather, the purpose of depreciation is an economic one and must remain so. Specifically, its purpose is to provide sufficient funds to acquire replacement machinery of equal value when the old machinery has exhausted its useful life.

The above example should illustrate satisfactorily the deterioration of cost calculation since the onset of inflation. No doubt I need not emphasize that industry unknowingly donates millions to consumers in this way every day. Weighed against these losses, the various special cost surcharges that many industries are already instinctively undertaking scarcely tip the scales. The so adamantly opposed Reich emergency tax is only a trifle compared to such huge losses.

Of course depreciation that is calculated for costing must be accumulated in the accounts, where it makes absolutely no difference whether it offsets the related asset account or is credited to a replacement reserve. To avoid accumulated amounts appearing to be greater than related assets and to allow a true picture of asset values, it would seem advisable to restate asset values in terms of paper marks and to credit the difference to a special contra account, say to a "Fixed Asset Valuation Account."

If things continue as before and people do not soon take a sober look at naked reality, many industries will face catastrophe in the not too distant future. In this respect, I would like to mention the new issues of stock that have become the order of the day. In my opinion the primary reason for these new issues is that companies have failed to provide adequate resources of their own to replace deteriorated pre-war assets. At the same time many of these companies, who are actually experiencing losses, have paid large dividends. In effect, then, they have distributed to their shareholders a portion of paid-in capital.

To what extent it is possible and advisable to increase prices is another question, especially considering the already diminished purchasing power of consumers and the current political atmosphere. That question has nothing to do with the question I have raised and treated strictly from a private sector point of view.

It is also quite possible that with close costing and accurate estimates of the useful lives of individual assets savings of a sufficient amount can be realized so that many companies will not have to raise prices despite the necessity of higher depreciation charges.   In any case, every conscientious and prudent businessman should account scrupulously for the condition and progress of production in his enterprise.   Too, it may not be feasible to ask German industry, which is already working under conditions of extreme difficulty, to make additional extraordinary sacrifices.

7. Faulty Cost Accounting*

Dr. Theodor Schulz,
Director of the Halle Salt Manufacturers Association

I.

In No. 234 of the *Industrie- und Handelszeitung* Mr. Gustav Kast made a number of statements under the above title that should not pass unchallenged. I unconditionally agree with several of his statements which I have taken the liberty to summarize and expand as follows:

1. The principle that only apples may be added to apples must continue to be observed in accounting for plant assets today.

2. From a purely private-sector point of view, depreciation is not intended merely to recover the historical cost of plant assets and should not be accounted for as if it were. Rather, the amount necessary to replace plant assets at the end of their useful lives must be set aside.

3. For this reason, under conditions of inflation, the prudent businessman should not continue to recognize depreciation using the same rate applied to historical cost. Depreciation should be increased in proportion to inflation, which finds expression in increased prices.

4. In calculating cost and setting prices, such increased depreciation should of course be taken into account.

5. The necessarily higher depreciation amounts should be charged to cost of goods sold, either openly or in some other form, so that their inclusion in the pricing process does not result in apparently higher profits which are then mistakenly distributed along with genuine profits.

6. Some way must be found to protect these increased depreciation amounts or reserves entirely or in part from taxation since they do not constitute reserves in the taxable sense, but normal depreciation charges. They are higher only because of changes in the value of money. Under present tax law, however, they would not go untaxed.

---

*   *Industrie- und Handelszeitung*, 5 November 1920, p. 1-2.

Of course the various principles underlying accounting are to be taken *cum grano salis*, for even before the war the value of money was never completely uniform. Even then (and this aside from cyclical fluctuations) the value of money sank perpetually, but so gradually and over such extended lengths of time that it was not perceived as such.

In 1880 a ton of coal in the Ruhr district cost on the average 4.55 M.; in 1885, 4.70 M.; in 1890, 7.98 M.; in 1895, 6.66 M.; in 1900, 8.53 M.; in 1905, 8.40 M.; in 1910, 9.78 M.; and in 1910, 11.56 M. The prices of other commodities rose in a similar manner.

This gradual decline in the value of money and the loss in purchasing power it entailed expressed itself correspondingly in wages, which approximately doubled during the same time period.

If one considers changes in the value of money due to individual cyclical swings in addition to the ongoing decline in the value of money, it becomes quite apparent that even before the war the value of money was never completely stable. Given two machines exactly alike, for example, one purchased in 1885 and the other five years later, the one purchased in 1885 will have been acquired substantially cheaper than the one five years later. The second machine, however, will have been charged to the plant and equipment account without correction for the value of either machine. And yet before the war no one would have objected that principle no. 1 above had been violated. The general decline in the value of money and the temporary fluctuations due to major business cycles were not restricted to Germany alone, but extended to most civilized countries.

Nevertheless, a company that acquired plant assets in 1880 and depreciated them at a rate of 10 percent per year for ten years will not have accumulated the amount necessary to purchase new machinery in 1890. Since even in normal times it is practically impossible to project the useful life of an asset (and thus the period over which it should be depreciated) as well as the amount necessary to replace it at the end of its useful life, every prudent businessman will have provided for depreciation in such generous amounts as to cover replacements to the extent humanly forseeable, be it by open depreciation or the creation of secret reserves.

The whole question only became of such extraordinary significance for the German businessman as a result of the outcome of the war and the after-effects of the revolution. After these events he had to deal with an adverse exchange rate as well as the almost equally serious steep inflation within Germany and the sharp increase in prices inflation brought about.

On the surface no difficulties arise in cost accounting if one views the matter as Herr Kast does in his example. Actually, however, the matter has rather a different color. Using Herr Kast's own example, if the machinery in question were acquired in 1913, the last year before the war, depreciation of 60,000 M. (6 x 10%) would have been recognized on the 100,000 gold-mark acquisition price in the six years since the outbreak of the war. If we assume further that the relationship of paper marks to gold marks is 1:10 as Herr Kast does, 4 x 10% = 40,000 gold marks = 400,000 paper marks would be depreciated over the remaining 4 years of an assumed 10 year useful life. If then the machinery has to be replaced at the end of the ten years, only 460,000 marks will have been set aside by means of depreciation while the new machinery costs one million paper marks. The calculation, therefore, was incorrect. In this case, extra depreciation in the amount of 235,000 M. annually (the 940,000 M. shortage divided by 4 years) would have to have been added.

The relationship, of course, will be so much the more favorable, the longer the expected useful life of the asset. A prerequisite for the accuracy of this calculation, however, is stability of the paper mark in the future. If the paper mark weakens and prices continue to rise, this amount will not suffice, and depreciation charges included in cost will have to be increased continually. But if the German economy begins to recover, even if not all at once, yet prior to the point at which replacement of the machinery becomes necessary, too much depreciation will have been charged. But this is the lesser of two evils since it will merely result in the creation of correspondingly large secret reserves.

There are no real difficulties, therefore, in charging appropriate depreciation amounts to cost calculation (assuming accurate computations). Of course the question remains whether or not the prices formed on the basis of these costs can be realized. If they cannot, the businessman will have to decide to what extent he can and is willing to mark down prices, that is, to what extent he is willing to assume the risk of sizeable cash shortages when he subsequently faces replacement of plant assets, which he will have to make up out of resources of his own or outside funds.

Turning to the question of how to account for the increased depreciation charges, Herr Kast's solution does not seem feasible. Indeed, in my opinion it meets with practical problems as well as legal ones. Legally the case is simple. According to the Commercial Code, §261, 2, joint-stock companies are to record plant assets at no more than acquisition cost or cost to manufacture. Now if, as Kast's approach unconditionally requires, one disregards the generally accepted principle of balance sheet continuity and aligns oneself with those theorists who contend that according to §40 of the Commercial Code assets depreciated at a substantially accelerated rate may be valued at current value at year-end, one would find oneself limited (relative to joint-stock companies) by §261, 2, in so far, that is, as current value is greater than acquisition cost or cost to manufacture. Returning to Kast's example:

Cost of the machinery in 1913	=	100,000 M.
Depreciation	=	60,000 M.
Book value	=	40,000 M.
Or, book value in paper marks	=	400,000 M.

But this restatement is not possible since according to §261, 2, the company in question can value the asset at no more than 100,000 M. A prerequisite for Kast's proposal, therefore, is amendment of the Commercial Code.

But I also see no possibility of due and proper implementation of this proposal from a practical point of view. What does paper mark mean? Nothing more than a concept that continually fluctuates. Of course foreign exchange rates and the prices of goods in relation to their pre-war prices provide reference points for the value of the paper mark. But which of the various possible relationships that exist simultaneously is the correct one? Foreign currencies cannot provide a basis since their value is subject to extreme fluctuations in a matter of days. Even the price of gold does not show absolute stability. The prices of plant assets show even greater differences. One need only consider the relatively small increases in the prices of real estate and farm land, etc., in comparison to the extraordinarily large increases in the prices of machinery, etc. How is anyone to achieve uniformity in the balance sheet under these conditions? One part of the balance sheet - say buildings - cannot be restated on the basis of an approximate increase in market value of 1:2 and another part - say machinery - on the basis of a ratio of 1:20.

The paper mark is simply not a stable concept; rather, its value fluctuates widely in relation to the gold mark. A substantial easing of our economic situation may bring about a rapid improvement in the value of the paper mark, so that by mid-year restated higher values lie far above actual market values.

Herr Kast's solution is only conceivable for a definitive restatement of assets after the mark has stabilized. But no well-managed company will think to restate assets after stabilization has occurred, in the same way no company thought to revalue assets upward again under normal, pre-war circumstances when those assets had been heavily depreciated and their book value no longer had any relationship to market value.

Some other method must be found to provide relief and security for enterprises, and in my opinion it must be just the opposite of Kast's.

Plant and equipment must continue to be valued in gold marks. At least a valuation method must be sought that is not based on today's sharply depreciated paper mark, but on values that presumably will serve as a permanent valuation basis after the economy recovers.

8. Faulty Cost Accounting[*]

Dr. rer. pol. Theodor Schulz,

Director of the Halle Salt Manufacturers Association

II.

As I mentioned in yesterday's exposition, the base value of gold did not always remain the same even before the war, but deteriorated gradually over the decades. If our economy recovers completely, furthermore, we probably never will return to the pre-war base value of money, but can expect prices to remain permanently higher than before the war. This assumption is reinforced by the facts that even in countries whose currency remains strong today prices have risen sharply and that in those countries too one cannot expect a return to pre-war price levels. Assume that in Germany we can expect a permanent doubling or tripling of prices and that for this reason there will be an average increase of 250% over pre-war prices: this percentage increase would, as it were, form the basis for the value of the gold mark in the future. As a result, all newly acquired assets, to the extent they are not cheaper (as is the case, for example, with land), would have to be recorded in the plant assets account at no more than 250% of their pre-war value. Any cost beyond that amount would be charged to expense. Of course this sudden write-off, which in some cases might prove sizeable, should not simply be expensed in a single month, but - when it is a matter of large sums - is more appropriately allocated over twelve months or, in some circumstances, over a longer period of time.

If, for example, a machine cost 1,000 M. before the war and 15,000 M. today, 2,500 M. should be debited to the asset account. The remaining 12,500 M. should be charged to a special balancing account, one twelfth of which should be amortized each month. In the present example, about 1,000 M. would be charged to expense monthly.

Of course it is quite conceivable that the year-end current value of a machine acquired in the middle of the year might prove less that the sum of the amount charged to plant assets plus the amount still in the special balancing account. If so, the loss would

---

[*]   *Industrie- und Handelszeitung*, 6 November 1920, p. 1-2.

have to be recognized retroactively at year-end before being incorporated in cost of goods manufactured. For this reason I recommend including from the outset of the fiscal year appropriate amounts in cost of goods manufactured for any plant assets acquired during the year and crediting those amounts to the special balancing account that contains the paper-mark excess cost. In this way a corresponding portion of the cost of assets acquired during the course of the year is covered in advance, yet overall the assets in question are recorded at their future gold-mark values, or at least at values no greater than their current values. Even the tax authorities will in the end find little fault with this principle if they consider it objectively since the provisions of the Commercial Code and the Reich Tax Code are based on normal economic circumstances with generally stable prices. If prices are not stable, the statutes (at least the tax laws governing the treatment and valuation of depreciation) must be changed to avoid the eventual ruin of a large portion of our enterprises - ruin that in many cases appears inevitable if the present laws are retained. Only we must be careful that the enacted laws not allow profits and genuine secret reserves over normal and necessary depreciation to escape taxation.

In addition, we must avoid in further negotiations with our enemies inaccurate conclusions concerning Germany's national wealth and the country's productivity and solvency because company balance sheets reflect extraordinary, paper-mark increases in the values of plant assets. [Valuing plant assets net of excess cost] would also provide a more reliable basis for determining the market value of stock as well as the credit-worthiness of enterprises. Such a reliable basis is lacking today because without these kinds of statutory provisions nonexperts are not able to distinguish between gold-mark values and paper-mark values in balance sheets nor to know what value to assign to the indefinite concept of a paper mark in individual cases. To illustrate, I need only refer to the remarks of the executive vice-president of Phoenix Mining and Steel, AG at the company's general shareholders' meeting, who expressly stated that the huge figures in the balance sheet were no indication of superior economic performance, but merely a result of inflation.

Hence, we must work toward either an agreement with the local tax authorities or general regulations on the part of the Reich tax authorities - enacted by statute if necessary - concerning the ratio at which plant assets are to be recorded and the increase in the percentage rate of depreciation for assets already on hand.

If the tax authorities do not accede, there is yet another possibility. The assumed 250% increase in value of newly acquired assets could be debited to the proper plant and equipment account and the amount in excess of that value could be debited to another asset account - say a Paper-Mark Excess Value Account - which would contain the excess values of all newly acquired plant assets and on which considerably higher depreciation would be recognized than on the ordinary accounts, this of course with the consent of the tax authorities or even as a matter of law. I am speaking here of percentage increases of 30-50% of the values originally recorded.

Of course in most cases this approach would require investment of considerable sums of new money. Indeed, at the moment new money is absolutely necessary in those situations in which too little depreciation has been recognized or insufficient secret reserves accumulated to cover completely the sharply increased costs of needed replacements. Besides, new capital not only serves to cover the increased cost of new plant and equipment, but to a large extent the extraordinary increase in working capital requirements. We must be careful later however (to the extent corresponding increases in prices are to be obtained) not to eliminate large segments of the economy by distributing profits (which are not profits at all). If markup on cost cannot always be realized, the way is still clear to allocate paper-mark excess values over an appropriately longer period of time. The time period involved should still be as short as possible and is necessarily limited by the least most acceptable return on capital. In any event, I believe that this approach would both clarify the balance sheet and render the balance sheet much more truthful.

We should even consider whether or not to demand statutory action to directly forbid recording full paper-mark values in the plant and equipment accounts and to fix instead maximum percentages of pre-war values for those accounts and make obligatory the recording of amounts in excess of those values in a Paper-Mark Excess Cost Account subject to increased depreciation. In this case all joint-stock companies who have recorded paper-mark values over the past few years must be required to remove amounts in excess of the probable future parity of the mark from the actual plant and equipment accounts and charged to the Paper-Mark Excess Cost Account or however one wishes to term it.

Depreciation recognized on plant assets originally recorded in gold marks, moreover, would have to be increased such that, as soon as it became necessary to replace the assets, either the necessary paper-mark amounts were on hand in full or largely so. In the former case, problems with the tax authorities would likely arise given the present demand for money on the part of the state. We simply have to point again and again to the importance of such increased depreciation on old gold-mark values for the national economy and the private sector. Indeed, it would be a rewarding task for the leading industrial organizations to muster all their means and bring about a change in the tax law regarding the valuation of depreciation.

The ideal procedure - and solely correct one from a private-sector point of view - would be to recognize depreciation great enough (as in the example I provided) that the means necessary to replace an asset would be available upon exhaustion of its useful life. Of course depreciation would very quickly (usually after only two or three years) attain and exceed present book value. But since it is not satisfactory to show assets with negative values, the only viable option is to establish an equivalent replacement fund for old gold-mark values among the liabilities. A precondition of this option, however, is a change in the law or at least express consent on the part of the authorities since §261, par. 3, of the Commercial Code no longer coincides with sound business principles under today's monetary conditions. Rather, it allows recognition of wear and tear on assets only in the form of depreciation or replacement reserves that reduce the value of an asset to 1 mark.

I doubt, however, that recognition of depreciation in the manner I have suggested will be sanctioned either statutorily or by consent of the tax authorities. But much would be accomplished if permission were given to increase depreciation on old gold-mark assets by an amount sufficient to accumulate expected replacement cost (based on projected future gold-mark parity), even if the increased rate of depreciation meant depreciating the asset to less than 1 mark. To remain with my example, expected replacement cost would be 250% of pre-war value. Thus, once an asset had been depreciated to 1 mark, an additional 150% would be needed in the replacement fund when replacement became necessary, and the additional allocations (as a minimum) would have to be tax exempt. As in the past, further increased allocations would continue to be possible in the future; those amounts, however, would be fully taxable. The measures I have suggested, therefore, should, in the interest of national economic recovery, be viewed as minimum provisions from the standpoint of commercial law; from the standpoint of taxation, on the other hand, they should be considered maximum provisions. The result would be that shareholders could lay no claim to such apparent profits as distributable profits.

9. Depreciation, Replacement and the Value of Money*
Richard Buxbaum

The inflationary shock waves that have shaken the foundations of the economy have brought to light a problem that actually already existed, but whose practical implications have become infinitely greater as the nominal values of real assets have increased out of all proportion. The problem can be formulated as follows: what is the meaning of depreciation from the businessman's point of view, and what provision for replacement of plant and equipment would seem prudent?

The immediate cause for renewed preoccupation with this question stems from the following fact: at the moment replacement of plant, machinery, and other equipment became necessary the businessman lacked the means to do so, which, as a result of inflation, had become rather sizeable. The question then arose as to whether, in light of the increase in prices, depreciation during the past several years should not have been greater. Frequently the question was posed well before the problem of replacement became acute and involved a careful assessment of future circumstances (tax considerations often played a role here).

What will be explored here then is whether or not a relationship exists between depreciation and the means expended to replace depreciated assets or even between depreciation and the means expended to acquire additional plant and equipment.

What is depreciation? The law has not provided a precise definition of the concept. In relation to the valuation of items in the balance sheet, the Commercial Code in §40 simply states the following:

> In entering inventory and other items in the balance sheet, one should value all assets and liabilities at values appropriate at the time the balance sheet is prepared. Receivables are to be valued at their probable net realizable value. Worthless receivables should be written off.

---

*   *Die Bank*, November 1920, pp. 686-96.

Depreciation here includes write-offs of assets that have become worthless. Since the function of adjusting asset balances for mere decreases in value can also be ascribed to the concept, it may be defined as follows: depreciation is the accounting expression of reductions in the values of assets.

Technically, depreciation can be recorded in two ways, either by a numerical reduction of the asset itself or by creating a contra account in the amount of the intended depreciation and retaining the original value of the asset. Thus, asset A, which has a useful life of 10 years, can be recorded after the first fiscal year either as A - A/10 = 9/10A, or the value of A can remain unchanged and a contra account in the amount of A/10 be created for valuation purposes. §261 of the Commercial Code contains the following provision for joint-stock companies:

> Plant and equipment and other items that are not intended for resale, but are devoted permanently to operations are to be valued at acquisition cost or cost to manufacture regardless of decline in value and an amount representing depreciation deducted or a corresponding amount entered in a replacement fund.

The valuation of items intended for resale, whether they have a market price or not, is generally accomplished by booking a direct loss to the account concerned (inventory, marketable securities, etc.). The difference between book value and value as prescribed by law is written off. The approach that calls for reduction of the value of the asset itself is ordinarily chosen for this purpose. In the case of plant and equipment, on the other hand, the formation of a contra account is usually preferred on grounds of clarity and ready overview.

Both a law from the pre-war era and a law that originated during the war clearly indicate that the definition of depreciation given above is in complete harmony with the tax laws. §13 of the (old) income tax law of 19 June 1906 reads in part as follows:

> Taxpayers who keep books according to the regulations of §§38ff. of the Commercial Code are to calculate profit . . . according to principles set forth in the Commercial Code for the valuation of inventory and accounting in general and in other respects according to sound business practice. These principles are to be followed in particular in regard to appreciation of fixed assets on the one

hand and annual depreciation on the other, insofar, that is, as it appropriately represents declines in value.

And §16 of the tax law of 21 June 1916 states that:

Business profit . . . is annual accounting profit calculated according to law and sound accounting principles. Depreciation is to be recognized to the extent it appropriately represents declines in value.

It follows from this understanding of depreciation that the concept only pertains to assets on hand (whose book value it determines) and that it never serves to fund new or replacement items. If provision is to be made for new plant and equipment, it can only be accomplished by creating a reserve fund in the amount of the acquisition price of the new plant and equipment. Depreciation does not have a thing to do with this reserve fund. It does not provide a measure of the amount required for such plant and equipment, nor does it in itself provide the means of acquiring the new plant and equipment.

Take for example a machine that cost 100,000 M. and has a useful life of ten years. For the enterprise this machine means an additional 10,000 M. in manufacturing costs. The total 100,000 M. are out-of-pocket costs and must be recouped through earnings. Normally these costs are recouped through sales of finished goods in the same manner as costs for materials, repairs, electricity, steam, coal, wages, salaries, etc. If the 100,000 M. are not included as expense all at once, but in ten equal installments, technically nothing is changed. The 100,000 marks are an operating cost, and after ten years they are used up, consumed, gone. Depreciation, therefore, cannot serve to acquire new plant and equipment; it can only express the gradual consumption of old plant and equipment.

Neither can one contend that depreciation in any way serves to "accumulate" funds, as several of the authors cited below do. Indeed, depreciation cannot fund an amount equal to the value of the old depreciable plant and equipment.

If the machine in the above example is labeled M, cash on hand K, all other assets A, and all liabilities and equities P, then *ceteris paribus* the following equations result:

Opening balance sheet: A + K = P.

After acquisition of the machine: A + (K - 100,000) + M = P.

If one were to write off the machine as worthless at the outset, the result would be a loss (V) of 100,000 M.: A + (K - 100,000) + V = P.

When the loss is distributed equally over ten years, one obtains the same result on the basis of the following equations:

Year 1: A + (K − 100,000) + (M − 10,000) + V = P, where V = 10,000 M.;

Year 2: A + (K − 100,000) + (M − 20,000) + V = P, where V = 20,000 M.;

Year 3: A + (K − 100,000) + (M = 30,000) + V = P, where V = 30,000 M.; etc.

To be sure, if business is good, one may expect company earnings to cover the loss (along with other costs and losses) and provide a surplus in addition. But if this expectation is not met, a *de facto* loss results, that is, the value of assets decreases by the amount of the cost of the machine and capital diminishes correspondingly.

But if one understands the nature of depreciation, all doubts about the insufficient amount of depreciation recognized previously disappear. For these doubts resulted from the mistaken idea that new, many times more expensive acquisitions had to be covered by depreciation. In particular, some have asserted the necessity of restating all values still expressed in "gold marks" in terms of "paper marks" and of recognizing depreciation on the basis of the lesser value of paper. But this idea is not only impracticable, it is fundamentally incorrect.

First of all, gold marks and paper marks are not stable values but fluctuating values. A twofold measure of value would be replaced by another, certainly common denominator, but a rubber-like one.

Also overlooked is the fact that changes in prices are not only caused by declines in the value of money, but by a number of other factors as well. Thus, the restatement of a machine valued in gold marks would require answering the following two questions: a)

What is the value of the machine in gold marks today?   b) What paper-mark value corresponds to the gold-mark value so determined?

Finally, the restatement of gold-mark values in paper marks appears to have no practical significance. For if the values of assets are increased in the same proportion as depreciation, the effect remains the same. If a machine is depreciated 10% per year and the historical cost of the machine was 100,000 gold marks, depreciation amounts to 10,000 M. annually and the machine is fully depreciated in ten years. If the cost of the machine is recorded in the books at two million marks, depreciation amounts to 200,000 M. annually and the machine, once again, is fully depreciated in ten years.

Recently, a series of articles concerning the practical meaning of depreciation has contravened this line of thought and sought to consolidate the ideas of "depreciation" and "reserves". In an article entitled "Production Policy",[1] Walter Rathenau correctly recognized the dichotomous nature of the problem:

> The function of a sound business enterprise is not fulfilled if, in the course of a year, it has not profitably produced goods in the quantity planned. In addition, a business enterprise is required to provide for the maintenance and replacement of its plant and equipment. If it fails to do so, it exploits its plant predatorily, exhausts it, and soon ceases to exist. It provides for maintenance by immediately covering all losses and damages to its facilities from funds on hand. It provides for replacement by accumulating surplus funds over the years which it may use in case of need.

After these correct introductory remarks, however, he continues as follows:

> There are two methods of recording the annual reserve allocation. It can occur on the debit side of the balance sheet where it is expressed as a reduction of the book value of plant and equipment. The rate of reduction is based on experience and is termed depreciation. Alternatively, one can open an account on the credit side of the balance sheet and allocate an appropriate amount to it each year. Such an account is termed a replacement fund.

---

[1]   *Vossiche Zeitung*, No. 455, 15 September 1920.

This passage already uses the word "reserve" in the sense of depreciation. But the following lines seem even more confusing to me:

> Until recently the two long-standing conventions of depreciation and reserve allocation were considered equivalent. And they were as long as the value of money remained stable. The inadequacy of depreciation as compared to a reserve account became apparent only when our currency began to lose value. Depreciation can only be recognized to the extent of book value. Reserve allocations, on the other hand, may exceed book value many times over. And since we cannot hope for a return to a stable currency for some time, the excess allocation will be necessary in the future. From an accounting standpoint, then, the problem can no longer be met with depreciation.

The technical difference between depreciation and reserve formation is not recognized in this passage. Inflation has nothing to do with depreciation; even before inflation depreciation could never exceed book value since it only functions to amortize historical cost. Inflation only has an effect on replacement fund allocations.

The same error occurs in an article published in the *Berliner Tageblatt*,[2] where the following statement is made:

> It is the same with the other question as to whether and to what extent the in part considerable sums, which previously were regarded as extraordinary write-downs and genuine reserves, are sufficient to cover the effective consumption of plant and equipment.

And another passage speaks of the fact

> that business enterprises . . . have not set aside, by means of a corrective account on the credit side of the balance sheet, enough of their own means toward replacement of worn-out plant and equipment.

When the author remarks that "the simplest way would be restatement in terms of paper marks", he overlooks the fact that multiplication of the values of plant and

---

[2]   "Falsche Bilanzierungsmethoden seit der Valutaentwertung" (Incorrect Methods of Accounting Since the Inception of Inflation) by Gustav Kast, 16 October 1920.

equipment (to express them in paper marks) along with a corresponding increase in depreciation gives exactly the same result.

Professor W. Prion discusses the same problem in two different articles.[3] Although he views the concept of depreciation essentially as I have defined it above, he arrives at incorrect conclusions. First he states quite correctly:

> The simple idea that a sufficient amount of each year's sales must be set aside to cover the acquisition or reproduction cost of replacement plant and equipment underlies the businessman's overall recognition of depreciation on "permanent" plant and equipment.

Later, however, he believes that depreciated amounts are accumulated and used for acquisition of new assets.

Professor Schlesinger,[4] too, presupposes that the amount necessary to acquire a new machine is available after an old machine has been depreciated. Of course he defines depreciation entirely differently than has been done so here. His definition of depreciation is "savings set aside for preservation of the enterprise by means of timely and appropriate replacement of plant facilities; savings in an amount that will allow on-going repair or replacement of plant and equipment normally on hand."

This is an explanation of depreciation that strains the meaning of the word itself. Rather, it contains all the characteristics of a reserve. But even if one accepted this definition, it would remain a mystery how the value of plant and equipment was to decrease and disappear from the books since depreciation is only supposed to serve as a savings account for new expenditures. It is also difficult to understand how Schlesinger bases the value of depreciation in this sense on the value of the old machine and not on the value of the machine to be acquired.

Depreciation and reserves are simply completely different things. The former relates to facilities on hand; the latter, to future facilities. The former may be effected by

---

[3] "Abschreibungen und Geldentwertung" (Depreciation and Inflation), *Plutus*, 15 September 1920 [reproduced as article # 1]; "Die Anlagen wirtschaftlicher Betriebe und die Geldentwertung" (Plant and Equipment of Business Enterprises and Inflation), *Deutsche Wirtschaftszeitung*, 1 October 1920.

[4] "Abschreibung oder Ersatz" (Depreciation or Replacement), *Werkstatttechnik*, 1 October 1920 [reproduced as article # 5].

decreasing the balance of the asset itself or by creating a valuation account with a credit balance. The latter, however, can only be effected by creating a reserve fund, which also carries a credit balance. Rehm (*Balance Sheets of Stock Companies*, 1914, p. 233) asserts that "depreciation and reserve funds are a contradiction."

The frequent confusion of these concepts and the measurement of reserve allocations according to depreciation seems to me to stem from the realization that the situation would become impossible if one were actually to create reserves for all future special requirements. But this very idea proves again the absurdity of treating depreciation and reserves alike.

Consider the reserves of an enterprise that is forced to shut down a portion of its plant or that rearranges its plant to manufacture a different product or use a new process. Could Krupp use the value of cannon lathes, drilling machines, and other machines used in the production of weapons to measure replacement reserves if it began manufacturing furniture, typewriters, automobiles, locomotives, and other items instead of weapons? Doesn't that seem impossible as well as absurd? And besides, would not reserves for all future requirements also entail anticipatory reserves for increases in wages, salaries, raw materials, electricity and power, etc., the costs of which have risen continually and by no small amount in the past few years.

The principles to which we are compelled to adhere, therefore, are:

1. depreciation is the accounting expression for declines in the value of assets, and

2. reserves represent the appropriation of funds for future needs.

Now we can approach the question of the extent to which reserves are admissible from a legal, sound business, and tax point of view.

With respect to the law, §262 of the Commercial Code requires joint-stock companies to form a "reserve fund" to cover accounting losses. Voluntary reserves, however, are also allowed if company bylaws permit them. They can even be adopted at general stockholders' meetings. At least one can conclude from §271 of the Code, which associates the right to contest such resolutions with an agreement of one twentieth of the stockholders, that the law encourages the formation of voluntary reserves in this manner (see also Staub's *Commentary to the Commercial Code*, 1906, vol. 1, p. 909). But there is no reason to assume that other legal forms of business may not also form reserves for losses or other specific purposes. Such reserves may relate to liabilities already incurred or to expected or contingent liabilities. The basic principle must always be to measure the objective value of the enterprise. The objective value of the enterprise, however, is not merely the difference between debits and credits in the sense of liabilities and capital, but "the value the enterprise has in the eyes of a purchaser who has considered all possible circumstances and who intends to continue operations".[5] §139 of the Reich Tax Code of 13 December 1919 states:

> In valuing assets devoted to operations in a business, one generally assumes that the business will continue after it is sold.

Hochschild, in the above cited article, correctly observes that

> anyone who continues the operations of a business onc purchases knows that one not only acquires existing debits and credits, but all encumbrances that may influence potential profitability. These future encumbrances already depress sales price even if they do not represent legal obligations due today.
>
> They are discounted in advance without any particular asset being written down . . .

In the same passage Hochschild cites a remark by Strutz[6] which is intended to show how far one can go with reserves of the type described. The remark reads:

> Thus, there is no reason for objection if depreciation recognized on individual asset accounts or allocations to valuation accounts are increased in anticipation of large expenditures for unproductive wages that may be expected to reduce net income sharply; insofar, that is, as this circumstance appears reasonably likely to depress the market value of the enterprise.

---

5   Dr. Hochschild, Frankfurt am Main, *Frankfurter Zeitung*, 16 January 1920.
6   *Deutsches Steuerblatt*, 1919, p. 391.

In my opinion, to be sure, the admissibility of such a reserve is questionable. Although Dr. Hachenburg (Mannheim)[7] views things somewhat more narrowly, he, too, states that

> lean years follow fat ones. He (the prudent businessman) will create reserves against the future whether he is the manager of a joint-stock company or is a single proprietor. He then lives off the reserves in unprofitable times.

I should like to consider it herewith proved that the law, both in spirit and as construed by well-known jurists, allows the formation of reserves for extraordinary future expenditures, as, for example, in the case of future acquisitions of plant and equipment. The magnitude of the reserves may be limited by accumulating expected future expenditures in annual installments. Since prices are subject to sharp fluctuations at present, it is understandable that opinions about amounts required also vary. Especially large allocations may well be justified in these times of sharp price increases and extremely favorable operating results.

From the standpoint of the private businessman, the shareholder who only temporarily invests in a company appears to suffer if reserves are formed from otherwise distributable earnings. But even this type of investor, that is, one who only seeks to make speculative profits, may more than cover his costs. For the price of a company's stock usually rises if the company accounts prudently and sets aside a portion of its income against the future. But the true representatives of the company are those shareholders who take an ongoing interest in the development of the company and for whom the avoidance of major setbacks is more important than the greatest possible dividend distribution to shareholders. Of course these sober-minded shareholders will demand that reserves be limited to amounts that accord with the spirit of the law.

One should also note for costing purposes that increased reserve allocations are a factor in seeking higher sales prices and greater profit figures; that, accordingly, allocations that are set aside for the future, but that burden profits today actually must be earned today by means of higher prices. The premium, furthermore, must be increased the

---

[7]   *Frankfurter Zeitung*, 16 December 1917, morning edition.

closer the time comes to install new plant and equipment. Perhaps in this way the goal can best be obtained that leading newspapers[8] have advocated regarding the adjustment of prices to the depreciated value of money, that is, that they not adjust all at once, but gradually. The question of reserves becomes more difficult from the point of view of taxes (just as does the question of supernormal depreciation). From this standpoint it is not a matter of the businessman's expectations concerning future conditions, but of merely "reporting correct values as of today. If lower values are reported, hidden reserves are contained in the valuation accounts and must be allowed for in the calculation of earnings (Prussian Higher Administrative Court)".[9] Further:

> Depreciation that reduces the value of assets below their fair market value is inadmissible and is to be treated as the formation of taxable reserves (Prussian Higher Administrative Court); §48 of the Regulations of the Federal Council, furthermore, reads as follows: Only those balance sheet accounts . . . may be considered true reserve accounts that can be shown to represent capital accumulation over and above stock capital (e. g., the statutory reserve funds, voluntary reserve funds, the dividend equalization reserve, reserves for contingencies), but not accounts that compensate for declines in the value of company assets (replacement funds) or cover liabilities already incurred (e.g., talon tax reserves, litigation reserves) or reserves established by insurance companies for insured values or for excess premiums to be returned to the insured as so-called dividends.

Be that as it may, it is not out of the question that tax legislation will eventually change direction and recognize as legitimate depreciation and reserves already considered admissible and necessary from business and legal points of view. The depreciation and reserves in question tend to stabilize reported earnings, an effect that certainly benefits the economy. One may also recall that the tax authorities raised no objection when, after the outbreak of war, a number of companies, in the interest of avoiding financial convulsions, reported profits out of all proportion to the times by tapping their reserves. Future tax legislation, furthermore, could be based on an idea that has already found expression in the law concerning the Reich emergency tax; the idea, namely, of leaving open the

---

[8]   Cf. *Frankfurter Zeitung*, 23 September 1920, No. 706, and 24 September 1920, No. 709; also *Berliner Tageblatt*, 16 September 1920, No. 437.

[9]   Strutz, *Kommentar zum Kriegssteuergesetz*, 1917, pp. 345-6, 394.

possibility of subsequent correction of the amount assessed. §56 of this law reads as follows:

> In case of too high or too low an assessment for property tax purposes, corrections and reassessments may take place within three years without new facts or supporting evidence justifying the reassessment being established.

In any case it is advisable to account with utmost care and strictly in keeping with fact, legal requirements, and sound business practice. It is also prudent to designate the accounts in the balance sheet and earnings statement according to their purpose. It ought to be possible to divide the profit-and-loss calculation into three parts, one that relates to the past, one that relates to the present, and one that relates to the future (which would no doubt result in losses for the latter two calculations).

10. The Effect of Inflation on Cost Accounting*

Richard Buxbaum

Charlottenburg

[Editor's note:] In nos. 234, 252, and 253 of the *Industrie- und Handelszeitung*, we published two articles by Gustav Kast and Dr. Theodor Schulz on the subject of faulty cost accounting [reproduced herein as nos. 5, 7 and 8]. We received a large number of replies from our readership. The following exposition represents one of those replies, which we reprint here to further clarify the question and to conclude the discussion.

Kast's recommendation involves restating all pre-war plant asset values, that is, "gold mark values," in terms of "paper marks" and crediting the difference to a "Fixed Asset Valuation Account." It would then be possible to recognize depreciation on the basis of the higher values. In keeping with this recommendation, one can no doubt assume that all other debit and credit items are to be restated as well, although Kast did not expressly say so.

Dr. Schulz, on the other hand, points out that the concept of a paper mark is a fluctuating one and that companies cannot legally state the value of plant and equipment at amounts greater than acquisition cost or cost to manufacture. Rather, he assumes a base gold-mark value of 250% of pre-war value, which represents the increase in the general price level. In the case of acquisitions, any amounts paid in excess of the 250% are to be expensed within a short period of time, preferably by the end of the year. Depreciation is to be recognized on older plant assets on a similar basis so that after completely writing off the original asset the replacement fund will contain a surplus of 150% of the value written off.

Both plans seem totally impracticable to me. In part they are based on incorrect assumptions and in part on arbitrary assumptions. At bottom is the idea that the mark of yesterday (the gold mark) is something so entirely different from the mark of today (the paper mark) that they cannot be summed. Certainly the difference gives rise to an undesirable impairment of clarity, an aesthetic shortcoming, albeit not a fundamental one. For just as one can add small apples and large apples if not apples and pears, one can add

---

*   *Industrie- und Handelszeitung*, No. 273, 1 December 1920, pp. 1-2.

mark amounts of varying value if not, say, marks, real estate, and machinery. Besides, assets and liabilities stemming from previous years have a tendency to compensate for today's depreciated currency. In part, they fall short of doing so by only a small margin (land account, building account); in part, they compensate completely (receivables, payables, mortgages, dividends in arrears, etc.).

Aside from the problem that these small differences would cause for restatement, the fact that no one can find a standard measure for the value of the mark makes it quite impossible. Even if one used exchange rates nothing would be accomplished. They fluctuate much too wildly. I need only cite a few exchange rate quotes for the American dollar during 1920: 2 January, 49; 9 February, 104.75; 26 May, 31.40; 15 November, ca. 84; on the next day, ca. 75; on 22 November, 66. In light of these differences, it should be readily apparent that for practical reasons alone it is better to avoid restatement on the basis of such a sensitive and variable denominator. But it is also fundamentally incorrect. If, namely, all balance sheet positions, debits and credits included, are restated in terms of another measure of value, the relationship of depreciation to plant assets remains unchanged. Whether I recognize depreciation of 10,000 M. a year on a machine with a book value of 100,000 M. or 20,000 M. on a machine whose value I have increased to 200,000 M. makes no difference; the outcome is the same. In both cases, the book value of the machine has been completely amortized after ten years. A proposal merely to increase the value of plant and equipment by the nominal, inflationary increase in prices violates the most basic rules of mathematics. Such an incorrect calculation is out of the question.

Also out of the question is the proposal to restate in terms of gold marks. For the assumption that the future value of gold will be 2½ times its pre-war value is completely arbitrary and cannot be proved. Besides, little is accomplished if, as described above, extra depreciation of 150% is recognized on old plant assets while replacement cost is perhaps 30 or 50 times the original value. In addition, individual years will be burdened with enormous expenses that can jeopardize the ability of the enterprise to compete with other enterprises for whom the problem of asset replacement has not yet become acute.

The matter clears up completely if one understands the purpose of depreciation correctly. The purpose of depreciation is by no means - as the authors of the two above-mentioned articles assert - to accumulate the means to replace old plant assets with assets of equal value after the old ones have exhausted their usefulness. Rather, according to law (§40 of the Commercial Code) depreciation serves to eliminate debit positions that have become valueless and to reflect declines in value of pieces of property.

Technically, depreciation can be recognized either by reducing the value of debit items or by creating replacement funds on the credit side of the balance sheet and leaving the original value of assets unchanged. In either case, it can never amount to more than the fully amortized book value of the related asset. By definition it can only relate to values on hand, never to future values. Seen in this light, no possible doubt remains as to how depreciation should be measured. Book value less residual value divided by the number of years of its useful life yields annual depreciation.

Looking at depreciation in this manner also clarifies a second question, that is, how to account for and to include in cost calculations the special requirements of the future. It seems both justified and necessary to include in cost calculations the extraordinary costs an enterprise expects to incur as soon as those costs can be estimated. Thus, if a machine that cost 100,000 M. in 1913 must be replaced in 1923, the customary depreciation of 10,000 M. a year must first be recognized. In addition, an allocation to reserve for the excess cost to be paid in 1923 is necessary and must be recognized for costing purposes. Suppose that it becomes apparent in 1918 that a new machine will cost two million marks. For the next five years an additional amount of 1,900,000 M. will be charged to account by allocating 380,000 M. per year to reserve. Whether or not allocation will proceed precisely according to this rule depends on three circumstances: the estimate of future acquisition cost (which is subject to frequent revision), the length of time before replacement becomes necessary, and the profitability of the enterprise in question.

It can happen that the estimate of future acquisition cost varies widely so that one year an increased allocation to reserve is required and another year no allocation is required at all. In general, moreover, it is not advisable to set aside the entire additional cost in one or two years if inflation and thus the necessity to create a reserve arises shortly before the point of replacement. It is better to allocate reasonable amounts to reserve during the brief period just prior to replacement and to recognize increased depreciation on total book value later. Of course, the size of the allocation is heavily influenced by the amount of desired profit. It would seem thoroughly economical to accumulate sizeable reserves in profitable years and thereby decrease risks in ensuing bad years.

Depreciation, accordingly, is the accounting expression of decreases in the value of assets, while the provision of funds for future requirements gives rise to allocations to reserves. Unquestionably we can only base cost calculations on these allocations if we are convinced that the formation of such reserves are justified and admissible. I can only touch on the question here and will do so from a legal, private-enterprise, and tax point of view.

As regards the law, §262 of the Commercial Code governs the formation of a reserve fund for joint-stock companies to cover accounting losses. In addition to this obligatory account, voluntary reserves are also permitted when companies' articles of incorporation provide for them. According to law as I interpret it, the balance sheet is supposed to express the objective value of an enterprise. By objective value I mean the value the enterprise would have for a purchaser who wishes to continue operations, but who carefully weighs all the positive and negative aspects. The presentation of this value, however, requires reserves of various kinds, not only for individual assets, but for the enterprise as a whole as well.

From the standpoint of the private sector, allocations to reserve in the above sense are justified because the reasons for price increases lie in the present, although as a practical matter the increases will take effect only in the future, that is, when new plant assets are purchased. It is, however, correct to include tomorrow's increased costs in today's revenues by incorporating them in sales prices since at the moment of the actual expenditure market conditions may have changed considerably.

From a tax standpoint the admissibility of such reserves is disputed. But we must work toward gaining recognition on the part of the tax authorities for these reserves and depreciation, which from a business and legal point of view are necessary and permissible.

In addition, subsequent correction in the manner of §56 of the Reich Emergency Tax Law should be made possible.

If reserves of the type described above are not allowed, selling cheap in times of rising prices will frequently prove necessary since cost will be based on old plant asset values. The high costs of new plant assets will then be subject to depreciation (and thus a factor in cost calculation) at a time when, say, the enterprise is forced to reduce sales prices because business is down.

If, however, depreciation and allocations to reserve as I have described them are not undertaken mechanically, but deliberately and from the general points of view mentioned at the outset, appropriate adjustment of sales prices to prevailing conditions will always be possible. That an increase in sales prices today in anticipation of future requirements can be justified as a matter of principle was established above. Too sharp an increase in prices generally will be prevented for reasons of competitiveness since the enterprise might otherwise jeopardize its market share.

Besides, all of today's charges benefit the future in any event. The anticipatory allocations to reserve will be discontinued once depreciation on replacement assets begins. As a result, price reductions in the future will compensate for price increases today.

I have limited myself here to merely indicating the direction in which cost accounting should move. In many cases cost accountants will not be able to work with firm numbers, but will have to depend on estimates. Yet they will be able to fulfill their function if the estimates are based on a correct understanding of the matter and if their approach is one that looks beyond the merely mechanical aspects of costing to the welfare of the economy at large.

C. The Organic Balance Sheet[*]
Fritz Schmidt

What will become apparent in the course of our discussion of the effects of the enterprise on the economy and, vice versa, the effect of the market on the enterprise, is the necessity of strictly separating asset valuation and income calculation. In a market economy, an enterprise is, as it were, adrift in a stream of values, floating in it and with it and even constituting a part of it. Our task is to find a method of accounting that allows us to bring to light the changes in value that eddy about the floating enterprise. The enterprise as a unit is not a rigidly fixed entity, which, standing stalwart in the economy, draws values from a rising and falling stream and returns them at the same or some other level. Rather, the metaphor is more accurate if one imagines the enterprise afloat in the economy, drawing values from those strata to which its managers gravitate depending on their cleverness or lack of cleverness and exchanging them for new values at advantage or disadvantage.

The point of departure for all values is market price. Market price affects the valuation of assets much as it affects production and profit. All the goods whose cost lies below selling price stream across the threshold of the market daily, hourly. Every shift at the threshold of a specific market or the market in general signifies a price-level change in the economy. If the price level is at first uniform for all goods, then any upward movement represents an increase in the value of all goods and any downward movement a decrease in the value of all goods. We know that the price level may rise generally; we know as well that general price-level movements never rise or fall uniformly since the utility values of individual consumers are at the bottom of things. The businessman's task is to navigate his little ship, that is, his enterprise, through these changes in value so that it achieves and maintains the highest degree of buoyancy. In other words, he is to put his enterprise together from values that have buoyancy, show a tendency to increase their relative value, and affect results so that the lowest possible costs always permit enterprise values to cross the threshold of the market.

[*]   Extract from Fritz Schmidt, *Die organische Bilanz im Rahmen der Wirtschaft*, 1921, pp. 59-61; 65-100.

Market price provides the measure of value for both consumer goods and capital goods. Once so valued, the former disappear from the market; the latter continue to exist as assets and may appear on the market again at any time during their remaining life. And even if they do not appear on the market again, current market price provides a basis for determining their market value. Current market price is the value the enterprise is to use in accounting for fixed assets. It is replacement value, and if calculated for all plant assets, including organization and start-up costs, it represents the reproduction value of the normal enterprise. The current market value of plant assets is the highest price the most marginal enterprise can pay and still earn (1) a normal return on capital and (2) entrepreneurial compensation. It is that amount that only allows enterprises to earn a supernormal profit if they operate at above normal efficiency. Reproduction value is always linked to the market. It vacillates with every price-level change and thus provides enterprise assets with a measure of price (one that has the advantage of being uniform for all enterprises) against which enterprise economy can be measured.

a) ACCOUNTING FOR ASSETS

1. Accounting for Tangible Assets *(Reproduction Value)*

The basis for accounting for tangible assets is current market value. Using this value greatly simplifies matters since this uniform measure of value is easily obtainable. There may be exceptions if for some artificial or natural reason there is no market for an asset. Such difficulties deserve attention, but we can ignore them for the time being since we only want to consider basic principles.

The objective of accounting for tangible assets is to determine the combined value of all enterprise assets and equities. This valuation is achieved by valuing individual balance sheet items at market price. The result expresses expenses and assets in terms of an enterprise earning a normal return. Not all enterprise assets, however, should be included; only those that contribute to the success of the working entity. Not includible are excessive accumulations of cash, securities, merchandise, and fixed assets not essential to the enterprise itself. One may account for them in a supplementary schedule if they are not excluded entirely. Idle fixed assets in particular should not be included without being designated as such. They have no value for the enterprise; it can earn no return on them.

Competition on the part of more suitably equipped enterprises assures that no return can be earned on excessive plant and equipment and brings about their transfer and utilization in other lines of production that do promise a return. They should not even appear among enterprise assets at scrap value.

As was the case in our discussion of the nature of inflation [in a previous chapter], it is important to distinguish between real assets and monetary assets when valuing items individually. On the liabilities side of the balance sheet, the distinction must be made between liabilities on the one hand and equity capital on the other.

a) Accounting for Monetary Items

Monetary assets and liabilities can be categorized into (1) cash holdings, (2) receivables and payables, and (3) interest-bearing claims, which may be assets or liabilities. Characteristic of the first two categories is that their nominal values are fixed. This characteristic is most apparent in the case of cash. Nominally, cash remains the same number of units regardless of any change in the price level. Of course this says nothing about the value of money itself. To the extent money constitutes a good in itself, such as in the days of metal currencies or even in the days of barter when money took the form of grain, livestock, etc., it represents a real value and is affected by changes in the price level in the same way as the good. Its value, then, would move in proportion to the values of all goods if costs and prices also moved in proportion. But since a uniformly proportional shift in utility values occurs only very rarely, real-value money would be subject to specific changes in value as well. As an example one need only consider the neutral countries which were plagued with huge inflows of gold during the war and suffered monetary inflation as a result of gold inflation. In my opinion, now that money is no longer tied to the value of gold in Germany, it is not wise to advocate gold as the measure of value in German balance sheets. I believe it is inadvisable because changes in the value of one good would determine the value of all goods. The one good (gold) is no longer a constituent part of the circulation of income, but depends on happenstance for its value. In particular, the value of gold depends on exchange rate developments; for under conditions of free arbitrage, it follows the rates that are most favorable at the moment. The value of any other good could be used as the standard of measure with equal justification.[1] In the end, the deciding measure is always current market price, the price level of the current production period being the price level against which all economic activity should be measured.

Today, in the days of a paper currency (whose introduction has opened the doors to unrestrained inflation), the value of money in accounting still remains nominally constant. In its relationship to goods, to market price, however, the value of money is subject to much sharper fluctuations. If the prices of real goods rise, the same sum of money buys fewer and fewer goods; if prices fall, one can buy more goods with the same sum of money. And since an enterprise as a manufacturing or retail firm draws life from transforming money into goods through purchase and production and goods into money through sale, maintaining the same values in the balance sheet in face of this constant turnover becomes a central problem of asset valuation.

Changes in the value of money affect payables on the liabilities side of the balance sheet much as they do receivables on the asset side. If prices rise, the enterprise is able to repay a previously incurred debt from the sale of a smaller quantity of goods than it would have to have sold at the time the debt was incurred. If prices fall, a larger quantity of goods must be sold to repay the debt than one previously would have to have sold to receive the same amount.

I might also note that if interest does not accrue on a current basis the current value of receivables and payables differs from their nominal maturity value by the amount of interest due between date of valuation and maturity date. If interest does accrue on a current basis, everything that has been said about the effects of changing prices is still valid. Another factor, however, is involved, that is, the difference between the contract interest rate and the current market rate of interest. If the contract rate of interest is higher than the market rate of interest, the value of the claim will rise above its nominal value so much the more, the longer the high rate of interest runs and the later repayment is effected. Vice versa, if the contract rate of interest is less than the market rate, the

---

[1]   Cf. Mahlberg, *Bilanztechnik und Bewertung bei schwankender Währung*, Betriebs- und finanzwirtschaftliche Forschungen, Leipzig, 1921. Mahlberg attempts to solve the problem of the value of money by tying values in the balance sheet to the value of gold. From the organic point of view, doing so too easily veils specific price-level changes. The method, which is founded in monetary theory, does appear well-suited for eliminating the main effects of inflation.

difference decreases the value of the claim so much the more, the longer the difference remains in effect and the later nominal repayment is made. In addition, risk plays a role in the value of the claim. The more uncertain the repayment, the less its value; and the later scheduled repayment date, the greater the possibility of failure to pay at maturity. These valuation factors manifest themselves in market price for fixed-rate securities that trade on an exchange. For trade notes receivable market price must be approximated.

The question arises here: is the change in the value of such a claim a change in the value of the claim or a component of income calculation, that is, a gain or a loss? If we consider all changes in value changes in the values of assets and account for those changes by debiting or crediting a capital adjustment account created for that purpose, they only affect income in that we expect that the enterprise should earn at least a normal rate of return on the higher or lower asset base. We do not expect any decreases in value to be replaced. By the same token, we cannot account for increases in value as income components either. In principle, this approach is correct with the exception of decreases in value that arise from credit transactions. If, for example, a line of production continually loses 2% of its accounts receivable, this 2% should be considered an expense. An actual increase or decrease in value because of economic conditions, on the other hand, is a change in the value of assets.

b) Accounting for Fixed Assets

The organic valuation of all fixed assets is market oriented and should focus on the date of the balance sheet, that is, the date on which replacement might ostensibly be required. Reproduction value of each piece of property, plant, and equipment at balance sheet date is the point of departure for the valuation of fixed assets. Full reproduction value must be considered in the case of completely new assets or unchanging, nondepreciable assets such as water power, land, etc. The effects of economic conditions on the changing value of individual fixed assets find ready expression in reproduction value, as, for example, when exploitation of electricity renders water power less valuable or a new invention renders a certain machine inferior. Of course, given the special character of fixed assets, their market value will not infrequently prove indeterminable. In that case an appraisal has to serve as replacement value. If the estimate of a fixed asset's value to the enterprise falls below its redeployment, liquidation, or residual value, it should be retired.

Depreciable assets should not be valued at full reproduction value, but at a value that takes into account depreciation to date. If a machine has a depreciable life of ten years and has already been used for five, it should be valued at only half of its reproduction value. The other half should be allocated to depreciation. (We will not consider the question of compound interest in this short exposition.) That the value of the enterprise changes as the fixed assets depreciate can only be mentioned here. It does not matter whether one chooses to depreciate fixed assets directly or uses a replacement fund. What is important is the effect of our use of reproduction value as of each balance sheet date. Then, if the price level changes, a different value will appear in each balance sheet. Consider the machine we mentioned that has a ten-year life and the following reproduction values on successive balance sheet dates:

Table 1 [*]

	Reprod- uction Value	Total Organic Depre- ciation	Organic Depre- ciation for Year	Organic Balance Sheet Value	Tradi- tional Depre- ciation	Trad- itional Balance Sheet Value
Beg. Yr. 1	10,000	-	-	10,000	-	10,000
End Yr. 1	20,000	2,000	2,000	18,000	1,000	9,000
" " 2	30,000	6,000	3,000	24,000	2,000	8,000
" " 3	40,000	12,000	4,000	28,000	3,000	7,000
" " 4	50,000	20,000	5,000	30,000	4,000	6,000
" " 5	60,000	30,000	6,000	30,000	5,000	5,000
" " 6	50,000	30,000	5,000	20,000	6,000	4,000
" " 7	40,000	28,000	4,000	12,000	7,000	3,000
" " 8	30,000	24,000	3,000	6,000	8,000	2,000
" " 9	20,000	18,000	2,000	2,000	9,000	1,000
" " 10	10,000	10,000	1,000	-	10,000	-
a	b	c	d	e	f	g

[*Table 4, p. 69 in the original]

In the balance sheet for each individual year, either the balance sheet values for the year (e) appear alone on the asset side or full reproduction values (b) appear on the asset side offset by the asset replacement fund [i.e., accumulated organic depreciation] (c) on the liabilities side. In this regard the organic balance sheet differs fundamentally from the traditional balance sheet. In traditional accounting, depreciation was embedded in an income figure subject to all the effects of changes in the value of money, and the asset replacement account summarized annual depreciation amounts of widely varying purchasing power in a meaningless total, which then served as a contra account to an historical cost figure that stemmed from yet another price level. In organic accounting, balance sheet values for fixed assets as well as depreciation are valued anew as of the date of each individual balance sheet. Columns **f** and **g** show the results of the traditional accounting treatment of fixed assets. First of all, the rigid retention of a fixed asset value assigned under vastly different conditions at some point in the past is not correct. It was correct at the time the asset was acquired. At that time it corresponded to reproduction cost. Every price-level change makes it incorrect; the number no longer represents the right value of the asset and no longer provides a measure for judging the profitability of the enterprise. That measure lies in the sum total of the current reproduction values of the enterprise. The total of the current reproduction values of an enterprise represents the current total value of plant assets that are necessary for production and on which the enterprise must recognize interest if it is to earn at least a normal return. Since fixed asset values serve as the basis for depreciation and depreciation assumes the greatest significance as a cost component, it is important to record fixed assets at their correct values. Their correct value, however, can only be the value that when charged to the goods produced during a production cycle, proves sufficient to replace in full at the close of the cycle the fixed assets consumed in producing the goods. Reproduction value must be used for this purpose as well.

The effect of the demands we place on accounting produces fixed asset accounts of a fundamentally different stamp than heretofore was the case. For, whereas traditional bookkeeping continues to cling to historical cost and makes allowance for changes in prices at best by means of special reserve accounts and whereas it does not recognize increases or decreases in value, but only gains and losses, we have developed a special approach to asset valuation. Under conditions of changing prices, the asset accounts themselves appear in the balance sheet at a different reproduction value each period as column **e** in the preceding table indicates. As a result, if the value of money is falling, the fixed asset accounts can increase in value severally and in total despite increasing depreciation. This is especially true for assets not subject to depreciation; their values will move much as those in column **b**. If the value of money increases, on the other hand, as is the case from the sixth year on in the example, asset values will fall below book value. According to the traditional view of the balance sheet, the decrease in value represents an expense to be charged to the current year's sales. From the organic standpoint, which views the enterprise holistically, the decrease in value is an aspect of asset valuation. Only annual depreciation amounts may be charged to individual periods. We will consider depreciation in our discussion of income determination.

If the traditional view of the balance sheet is deficient because it combines changes in the value of assets with income calculation, organic accounting, to avoid the same error, must create a special capital adjustment account to accumulate the changes in value that otherwise would appear in the profit-and-loss account. The above example can be extended to illustrate the formation of this account and its relationship to the fixed assets account. The example can be construed as one asset or fixed assets in total. (Cf. Table 2.)

The following figures for the fixed asset and capital adjustment accounts clearly demonstrate how asset values adapt to price-level changes in the organic balance sheet. At each fiscal year-end the current reproduction value of fixed assets appears on the asset side of the balance sheet and the capital adjustment account (which will be discussed below) on the liabilities side. According to the traditional view, any change in value would appear as gain or loss in the profit-and-loss account and would be treated as entrepreneurial profit or loss. The fact that this treatment is incorrect could be ignored during periods of relatively stable prices. Today's fluctuations in the value of money clearly demonstrate the indefensibility of this procedure. The greater the fluctuations and the greater the extent of enterprise fixed assets, the greater the changes in value and the riskier their incorrect treatment as profit or loss. Treating increases in value as profit as is done today entails especially serious risk. For as a result, capital may be distributed as dividends, income tax may be paid on increases in value, and businessmen may go to jail

Table 2[*]

Year	Fixed Asset Account				Capital Adjustment Account			
		M		*M*		*M*		*M*
1	Opening Balance Sheet Change in Asset Value	10,000 10,000	Ending Balance Sheet	20,000			Ending Balance Sheet	10,000	Fixed Asset Account	10,000
2	Opening Balance Sheet Change in Asset Value	20,000 10,000	Ending Balance Sheet	30,000	Ending Balance Sheet	20,000	Opening Balance Sheet Fixed Asset Account	10,000 10,000
3	Opening Balance Sheet Change in Asset Value	30,000 10,000	Ending Balance Sheet	40,000	Ending Balance Sheet	30,000	Opening Balance Sheet Fixed Asset Account	20,000 10,000
4	Opening Balance Sheet Change in Asset Value	40,000 10,000	Ending Balance Sheet	50,000	Ending Balance Sheet	40,000	Opening Balance Sheet Fixed Asset Account	30,000 10,000
5	Opening Balance Sheet Change in Asset Value	50,000 10,000	Ending Balance Sheet	60,000	Ending Balance Sheet	50,000	Opening Balance Sheet Fixed Asset Account	40,000 10,000
6	Opening Balance Sheet	60,000	Ending Balance Sheet Change in Asset Value	50,000 10,000	Fixed Asset Account Ending Balance Sheet	10,000 40,000	Opening Balance Sheet	50,000
7	Opening Balance Sheet	50,000	Ending Balance Sheet Change in Asset Value	40,000 10,000	Fixed Asset Account Ending Balance Sheet	10,000 30,000	Opening Balance Sheet	40,000
8	Opening Balance Sheet	40,000	Ending Balance Sheet Change in Asset Value	30,000 10,000	Fixed Asset Account Ending Balance Sheet	10,000 20,000	Opening Balance Sheet	30,000
9	Opening Balance Sheet	30,000	Ending Balance Sheet Change in Asset Value	20,000 10,000	Fixed Asset Account Ending Balance Sheet	10,000 10,000	Opening Balance Sheet	20,000
10	Opening Balance Sheet	20,000	Ending Balance Sheet Change in Asset Value	10,000 10,000	Fixed Asset Account Ending Balance Sheet	10,000	Opening Balance Sheet	10,000
11	Opening Balance Sheet	10,000	Ending Balance Sheet Change in Asset Value	5,000 5,000	Fixed Asset Account	5,000	Ending Balance	5,000

[*Table 5, p. 72 in the original]

as profiteers for attempting rightly and as good managers to maintain the value of their enterprise, which is one of their foremost responsibilities.

The capital adjustment account (or account to correct for changes in value) stands on the liabilities side of the balance sheet opposite the asset accounts (which contain current reproduction values).   Assume in the above example that the asset in question is nondepreciable.   Only if the price level does not change is no offsetting entry required when the asset is valued at current reproduction value.   But if the price level does change in the course of the accounting period, a credit to the capital adjustment account is required when prices are rising and a debit when prices are falling.   The credit or debit corresponds to the increase or decrease in the value of the one fixed asset or total fixed assets as the case may be.   All increases in value over and above acquisition cost are carried to the capital adjustment account, to which they become permanently attached. They only detach again if the value of the asset falls or the enterprise liquidates.   To date the law (Commercial Code, §261) has provided only a poor substitute for our clear distinction between increases in value and profit by prohibiting joint-stock companies from valuing assets above cost.   But the law does not prevent assets from being reported at too high values in subsequent years if the price level falls.   Organic accounting would show a decline in value in the balance sheet as well as an increase in value, and since the amount of the decline would not be debited to the profit-and-loss account, organic accounting would not report an unwarranted reduction in earnings.   Under these circumstances, the game played with so-called secret reserves could come to an end.   Generally, secret reserves do not represent reserves at all, but instinctively concealed increases in value, which businessmen have quite correctly sensed they should not report as profit.

The capital adjustment account can appear on the asset or liabilities side of the balance sheet.   When an asset is acquired, the new asset is entered in the accounts at current reproduction value, that is, at market value.   Its corresponding credit appears on the liabilities side of the balance sheet.   If acquired when the enterprise is founded, it appears at exactly the same amount among the liabilities or in owners' equity.   If the price level then rises, the value of the asset rises and, at the same time, the amount of the increase in the asset's value accumulates in the capital adjustment account.   This account serves as an adjunct account to owners' equity and thus adjusts owners' equity for the change in the price level. It can also occur as a contra account and offset owners' equity if, following a drop in the price level, the value of fixed assets declines. If, say, in year eleven the value of the asset in the above example fell below the original 10,000 M. paid for it to only 5,000 M., the accounts concerned would appear as follows:

Fixed Asset Account

Opening balance sheet	10,000	Ending balance sheet	5,000
		Capital adjustment	5,000

Capital Adjustment Account

Fixed assets	5,000	Ending balance sheet	5,000

Ending Balance Sheet

Fixed assets	5,000	Owners' equity	10,000
Capital adjustment	5,000		

The capital adjustment account now indicates a decline in the value of the enterprise, which, however, is not a disadvantage if the decline does not exceed the decline in the general price level.

The fixed asset account, valued at reproduction value as of the balance sheet date, in conjunction with the capital adjustment account brings the valuation of the assets and equities in line with the current price level. The question of the valuation of depreciation on revalued fixed assets, however, has remained open to this point. Traditional accounting indicates that there are two methods of depreciation. Either the amount of depreciation recognized is deducted directly from the fixed asset account and debited to profit and loss (the value of the asset declines by this amount), or an asset replacement account is established. The amount of depreciation recognized is then credited to this account at the same time it is debited to profit and loss. Both methods are also possible here, although the latter method is preferable because it more clearly shows the relationships.

We have already considered depreciation in our discussion and even calculated the appropriate amount in Table 1. The principle that governs depreciation from the organic view of the enterprise is that every production cycle must replace that portion of fixed assets actually consumed at current replacement cost as of the day of the close of the cycle. (We will have to consider depreciation again later as an essential cost component for costing purposes). It must be replacement cost at the end of the cycle, that is, as of the point in time when the means for replacement are realized in the sales price of the product. Only then can cost components be replaced, and if one wishes to realize replacement cost in full, depreciation must be exactly as high as the current cost to replace the assets consumed. Assume an enterprise uses straight-line depreciation and, to simplify matters further, that the enterprise operates ten machines of the same kind, each of which has a ten-year useful life and one of which must be replaced each year because of differing ages. That is, the enterprise begins with a set of machines that are 1, 2, 3, 4 through 10 years old. If the acquisition cost of each new machine amounted to 1,000 M., one would only pay 5,500 M. to replace all ten, which have been used on the average for 4½ years. That amount would be the beginning value of the machines and would be balanced by an equal amount of capital on the liabilities side of the balance sheet. If we used an asset replacement account, 10,000 M. would appear as the full value of the new assets in new condition, and the asset replacement account would contain 4,500 M. Thus, the opening balances would appear as follows:

Fixed Asset Account

Opening balance	10,000	

Capital Account

	Capital	5,500

Asset Replacement Account

	Opening balance	4,500

Now assume that the fixed assets undergo the various changes in value shown in Table 3.

Table 3[*]

	Fixed Assets at Reprod. Value	Capital Adjustment Account		Capital Account	Asset Replacement Account		Profit and Loss Account
					For Ret. F/A	For Accumulated Depreciation Plus Increases in Value	
	Dr.	Dr.	Cr.	Cr.	Dr.	Cr.	Dr.
Beg. yr. 1	10,000	-	-	5,500	-	4,500	-
End yr. 1	20,000	4,500	10,000	5,500	2,000	4,500 + 4,500 + 2,000	2,000
" " 2	30,000	9,000	20,000	5,500	3,000	4,500 + 9,000 + 3,000	3,000
" " 3	40,000	13,500	30,000	5,500	4,000	4,500 + 13,500 + 4,000	4,000
" " 4	50,000	18,000	40,000	5,500	5,000	4,500 + 18,000 + 5,000	5,000
" " 5	60,000	22,500	50,000	5,500	6,000	4,500 + 22,500 + 6,000	6,000
" " 6	50,000	18,000	40,000	5,500	5,000	4,500 + 18,000 + 5,000	5,000
" " 7	40,000	13,500	30,000	5,500	4,000	4,500 + 13,500 + 4,000	4,000
" " 8	30,000	9,000	20,000	5,500	3,000	4,500 + 9,000 + 3,000	3,000
" " 9	20,000	4,500	10,000	5,500	2,000	4,500 + 4,500 + 2,000	2,000
" " 10	10,000	-	-	5,500	1,000	4,500 - + 1,000	1,000
" " 11	5,000	5,000	2,250	5,500	500	4,500 - 2,500 + 500	500
	a	b	c	d	e	f	g	h

[*Table 5 [sic], p. 76 in the original]

The balance in the fixed assets account (**b**) represents the stock of fixed assets, including replacements, at current reproduction value.   The balance in the asset replacement account (**f** and **g**) represents accumulated depreciation for the 10 machines (45/100) at reproduction value.   The balance in the asset replacement account plus the balance in the capital account and the balance in the capital adjustment account equals the balance in the fixed assets account.   Worn out and unused fixed assets are debited to the asset replacement account when credited to the fixed assets account.   Annual depreciation is debited to the profit-and-loss account since it is an expense.   It is credited to the asset replacement account.   Acquisitions are debited to the fixed assets account and credited to cash.   The replacement values must equal the reserve.

This equality is the test of the correctness of the method, for only if accumulated depreciation exactly equals replacement cost are we in a position to pay for the replacement. But that is only the case if depreciation is calculated on the basis of the current reproduction value of fixed assets. We have simplified the discussion for the moment by assuming that at the end of each accounting period one of the ten machines is retired and replaced. And even when such straightforward replacement is not possible, the amount of sales set aside for depreciation is transformed as quickly as possible into fixed assets or merchandise.

The sequence of entries at the end of the third year, for example, would be as follows:

1. Writeoff of the worn out, retired machine at reproduction value.
   Dr. asset replacement account, cr. fixed asset account. 4,000 M.

2. Acquisition of the new machine = 4,000 M.
   Dr. fixed asset account, cr. cash. 4,000 M.

3. Recognition of depreciation for the period ended at reproduction value = 4,000 M.
   Dr. profit and loss, cr. asset replacement account. 4,000 M.

4. Recognition of the increase in value over the preceding year. 36,000 − 27,000 M. (for the nine remaining machines).
   Dr. fixed asset account, cr. capital adjustment account. 9,000 M.

5. Recognition of the increase in value for depreciation to date on total fixed assets at reproduction value = 18,000 − 13,500 M.
   Dr. capital adjustment account, cr. asset replacement account. 4,500 M.

6. Transfer of fixed assets including the replaced machine to the balance sheet at reproduction value.
   Dr. balance sheet account, cr. fixed assets = 40,000 M.

The cardinal principle of valuation in the organic balance sheet is valuation at market value as of balance sheet date (market value can be redeployment value if the market is saturated) in order to determine correct worth as of that moment. The fixed assets account and the asset replacement account conform to this principle in our example, although, of course, the two accounts could have been combined by deducting depreciation directly from the assets account. The fixed assets account shows the current total balance sheet value of the fixed assets; the amount contained in the asset replacement account is subtracted from that value to arrive at value as of the moment. The changes in value that are debited or credited to the fixed assets account at the end of each period are accumulated in the capital adjustment account. The balance in the capital adjustment account in the example gradually grew to reflect a maximum increase in value of 50,000 M. and then declined to zero as the price level fell. Indeed, in year 11 it declined to the point of becoming a deduction from capital. On the asset side, the same decline left a current value of only 5,000 M. in the fixed assets account. The 5,000 M. loss in value, however, was booked to the capital adjustment account.

The asset replacement account contains first of all the decline in value of 4,500 M. from the initial balance sheet, which equals that period's depreciation. To subscribe to the principle of depreciation, that is, to assume that the enterprise will continue to exist and thus should value its assets at reproduction value less accumulated depreciation rather than liquidation value, is also necessary in organic accounting. Depreciation itself, however, changes not only as a periodic amount, but in total if the point of departure is reproduction value. The change in value must also find expression in the capital adjustment account. Thus, whereas increases in fixed asset values are credited to the capital adjustment account, an amount must be debited on the other side of the equation that corresponds to depreciation on total value, to the content of the balance of the asset replacement account in relation to the fixed assets account. In other words, price-level changes affect the asset replacement account in exactly the same way as the fixed assets account. In fact, they affect it proportionately to the fixed assets account.

This relationship becomes much clearer if we consider the content of the asset replacement account. In our example, it corresponded to accumulated depreciation of 45% each period. Each year a machine was retired and a new one was purchased. If, however, the reproduction value of the entire ten machines rose from 10,000 to 60,000, the replacement value for 4½ used machines must rise from 4,500 to 27,000. Procedurally, this is accomplished by transferring the increase in value from the capital adjustment account. If the reproduction value of fixed assets falls, the value of the asset replacement account falls proportionately. Technically, this calls for a debit to the asset replacement account and a credit to the capital adjustment account.

Only if one creates a capital adjustment account, which could also be designated "account to correct for changes in value," is it possible to always maintain the equation "fixed assets account = capital account (original value attributable to fixed assets) + asset replacement account":

At the beginning of year 1:

10,000 fixed assets (dr.) = 5,500 capital (cr.) + 4,500 asset replacement (cr.).

At the end of year 1:

20,000 fixed assets (dr.) = 5,500 capital (cr.) + 5,500 capital adjustment (cr.) + 9,000 asset replacement (cr.).

At the end of year 5:

60,000 fixed assets (dr.) = 5,500 capital (cr.) + 27,500 capital adjustment (cr.) +27,000 asset replacement (cr.).

At the end of year 11:

5,000 fixed assets (dr.) = 5,500 capital (cr.) − 2,750 capital adjustment (dr.) + 2,250 asset replacement (cr.).

Only by means of the capital adjustment account, which corrects the capital account, does it become possible in bookkeeping to report correct asset values in the balance sheet. Until now this proposal has always failed because all changes in value were not recognized as such, but appeared as gains in the profit-and-loss account. Yet this treatment was instinctively understood to be incorrect, and accounting practices had to be developed that permanently concealed asset values. These practices have even been sanctioned by law in that joint-stock companies are required to value securities and inventories at no more than acquisition cost or cost to manufacture (Commercial Code,

§261, 1-3). This procedure may be tolerable when prices are stable, but it has a grotesque effect today. Today's balance sheets, which are made up of acquisition costs and costs to manufacture partly from the days of the stable gold mark and partly from various stages of inflation, are a terrible mess. Businessmen and bookkeepers can hardly make sense of them, not to speak of stockholders and other interested parties who have this mishmash served up to them primped and primed.[2] How clear a balance sheet would seem in comparison in which each asset appeared at its current value. The businessman may well place no particular importance on informing the public about his situation, but his interest in the matter lies elsewhere. He needs current values in order to manage. Only when he knows reproduction value is he able to judge whether or not he is operating successfully, that is, whether he includes fixed asset depreciation in the price of his product and still earns a profit.

c) Depreciation in particular

Correct valuation of fixed assets at current reproduction value is strictly necessary for valuing depreciation correctly. Depreciation is just as much a cost component question as it is one of declining fixed asset values due to wear and tear. For this reason, it could be discussed just as appropriately in relation to accounting for costs, where it could not be ignored in any case. Certainly the discussion to this point will make its consideration here in the framework of organic accounting easier. The measure of depreciation is wear and tear. In individual cases depreciation can only seldom be fully measured. Generally, one simply estimates the useful life of a fixed asset in the framework of enterprise operations and charges each period with replacement of a pro rata share of the value of the fixed asset over the asset's useful life. If a fixed asset will be consumed in five years, each year is responsible for one fifth of the replacement cost. The primary question then becomes how to measure these replacement costs. Their recovery occurs each time the enterprise sells its product. The proceeds from sale, or market price, contain an amount that represents recovery of fixed asset wear and tear caused by the manufacture of the goods sold. The first question we will address here is how much, from a purely business

---

[2]   Cf. Prion, *Die Finanzierung und Bilanz wirtschiftlicher Betribe*, 1921, p. 10f.

economics point of view, the remuneration must be to fully compensate for the consumption of the physical asset. We will then examine the extent to which a market economy permits such remuneration.

By right, recognition of depreciation must place the businessman in the position of maintaining the relative significance of his enterprise in the economy. He can only do so if the prices of his products provide enough remuneration to acquire at the moment of sale exactly the same quota of fixed assets that was consumed during the related production cycle. In the example above (Table 3), this requirement was taken into account with the insertion of the depreciation quotas under **g** and **h**. Each depreciation charge that represents the correct amount to be debited to profit and loss appears under **h**. The credit to the asset replacement account appears under **g**. The amount expended to replace the machine retired each year is debited to the fixed assets account and credited to cash. The latter transaction represents a feasible assumption that facilitates insight into the relationships described. The amount of depreciation required each period from a business economics point of view is decided by market conditions. It must represent the reproduction value of wear and tear if the enterprise is to be no better or worse off in the ensuing period.

Valuation of depreciation at reproduction cost, as business economics requires, harmonizes completely with the demands of the market. If the price level rises, market prices rise not only for consumer goods but for fixed assets as well. The businessman receives considerably higher revenues that give the appearance of much higher profits, which, however, actually contain increased depreciation quotas and other costs. The revenues are so high that even at the higher price level the enterprise earning a normal return is able to acquire new plant assets with the same capacity as those consumed and to pay the higher wages and materials prices of the new production cycle. Only that portion of revenue that exceeds the reproduction value of these costs is profit. Valuing depreciation and other costs at reproduction value allows maintenance of the relative value of the enterprise in the economy whether production is increasing or decreasing. During periods of decreased production with their increased prices and reduced inventories, one only has to replace the actual consumption of the preceding production cycle. In the current cycle, consumption diminishes along with the utilization of fixed assets, and the replacement requirements placed on later cycles diminish accordingly. When prices fall as a result of increased production, the lower prices facilitate plant expansion and thus more intense production. Recognition of the harmony between the demands of business economics and developments in the economy at large is the essence of the organic concept of the enterprise and balance sheet.

The reproduction value of depreciation, accordingly, necessarily fluctuates. If we assume as in our example above (Table 3, **f**, **g**, and **h**) machines with a ten-year useful life, one of which must be replaced each year, the purchase price of the replacement machine at the end of a production cycle corresponds to depreciation for that period of time. This amount changes with the price level. In the example it amounted to 1,000 M. at the beginning of the first year, 2,000 M. at the end of the first year, 6,000 M. at the end of the sixth year, and then sank to 500 M. at the end of the eleventh year. Annual depreciation, therefore, would have to vary to the same extent if the price level underwent these changes.

The traditional concept of the balance sheet is entirely inconsistent with the organic concept. The Commercial Code, §261, 3, specifies that fixed assets not intended for resale, but permanently dedicated to the business of the company may be entered at acquisition cost or cost to manufacture regardless of lower market value if depreciation in an amount equal to the decline in value is deducted from cost or credited to a replacement reserve. To be sure, the law is only binding for joint-stock companies, but almost all companies conform to it. According to the prevailing school of thought, that amount represents the upper limit for total depreciation on cost to manufacture, and the sum of individual depreciation charges should not be greater than or less than this amount. In our example, this would mean that 1,000 M. depreciation should be accumulated annually relative to fixed assets with a cost of 10,000 M. and an average useful life of 10 years, regardless of the replacement cost of the machine retired each year. During periods of stable prices, one can overlook the fact that this principle is completely incorrect because the historical cost of an old fixed asset and its current reproduction value are in fact practically identical. At present it is impossible to say another word in favor of this view, even if its application as required by law calls for depreciation of only 1,000 M. at, say, the end of the fifth year in our example. The remaining 5,000 M., which are normally recovered in the market price received, appear as profit, which, in turn, may be seized in full as war profits or substantially reduced as income and thus contributes greatly to the demise of the enterprise.

In contrast, a new school of accounting theorists who think along business economics lines tends more to recognize depreciation not on acquisition cost, but on replacement cost, which in the case of a long-lived asset may lie far in the future. Schmalenbach recognized the significance of replacement cost early on in his *Dynamic Accounting*,[3] but rejected it because at the time the shortcomings of historical cost as a basis for depreciation did not seem much greater than those of an imaginary replacement cost that simply could not be determined in advance. Prion[4] tells of methods in practice that suddenly shift from historical cost to replacement cost as a basis for depreciation and charge so much depreciation to the last few years of an asset's life that, together with the depreciation already recognized, it provides the full amount required in the asset replacement account to replace the asset at the appropriate time. Prion himself shrinks at the consequences, that is, at the high prices that would result when the price level was rising, and believes that national economic interests preclude the use of such a depreciation policy.

Mahlberg,[5] in his method of expressing all balance sheet values in terms of gold marks, also arrives at depreciation amounts whose spirit conforms to that of organic accounting. He, too, wants to record a price for fixed assets "which presumably will be current at point of replacement so that by the end of the useful life of the asset a sum will have been accumulated through depreciation sufficient for replacement."

The Union of German Machinery Manufacturers[6] has recommended the following for its members: 1. Depreciation or replacement charges should be adjusted so that the means required for replacement are available at point of replacement. 2. To the extent inflation has not been taken into account in calculating depreciation in previous years, the deficit should be considered in calculating depreciation or replacement charges.

---

[3]   Leipzig, 1920, p. 90f.
[4]   *loc cit.*, p. 44.
[5]   *loc cit.*, p. 52.
[6]   Bulletin No. 1, 1921. Charlottenburg 2, Hardenbergstr. 8.

These approaches contain various errors. Consider first an error contained in the approach of the Union of German Machinery Manufacturers. That organization recommends making up previously omitted depreciation in later years. To do so runs counter to the laws of the market. Every year can and does recover the correct depreciation charge in the prices of goods sold. If one fails to recognize it in full, that is, if one treats it as profit and distributes it, it can only be recouped from profits, which means reducing profits in later years.

The major error, however, is equating replacement value for depreciation purposes with replacement value as of actual replacement date. But that date always lies in the future, and not infrequently quite far in the future. It might at first seem reasonable to look to the future since the present, with its increased price level, has proved the inadequacy of historical cost as a basis for depreciation. But future replacement value is incorrect, too, because it measures the present with the wrong standard of measure (if, that is, a stable price level does not conceal its inadequacy). Besides, there is the difficulty of measuring future replacement values accurately. Fortunately, the organic nature of the economy is harmonious enough to spare the accountant the worry of incorrectly estimating a future value. Indeed, it prescribes the least troublesome of all values - current value - as the only correct one.

The mistake one makes in using historical cost as a basis for depreciation is in principle the same mistake one makes in using future replacement value. Both may lie above or below current replacement cost; for this reason depreciation based on either may be more or less than current replacement value calls for. The fact that the current value of fixed assets is the only correct basis for depreciation follows from a consideration of price-level changes. Assume the price level has risen five fold. If production remains the same, customers pay five times as much for depreciation [in the sales prices of goods], but exactly that, no more, no less. For if a businessman wants to value depreciation higher than it actually costs, he runs into the rock wall of the market. If he values depreciation too low, he reports the difference as profit, whereas it ought to represent replacement of fixed asset consumption.

If one wants to demonstrate the correctness of organic current value depreciation, what one must explain is that use of the method assures the relative position of the enterprise in the economy as a whole (provided an error in judgment on the part of the businessman does not jeopardize it). This consequence of our approach in particular requires explication, that is, that depreciating fixed assets on the basis of current cost, despite the fact that total depreciation corresponds to neither acquisition price nor future replacement cost, safeguards the relative value of the enterprise. Take as an example one of the machines we have already mentioned. Historical cost was 1,000 M. and future replacement value 10,000 M. (or one can imagine the significance of these amounts reversed). Consider then the effect of the widely fluctuating, transitory replacement values over the course of the machine's ten-year useful life (cf. Table 4).

Table 4[*]

| I Historical Cost or Future Replacement Value | | II | | | | | |
| Depreciation on the Basis of Historical Cost | | Current Replacement Value | | | Organic Depreciation | | |
a)1,000	b)10,000	a) Rising	b) Falling	c) Chang.	a)	b)	c)
End Yr 1 100	1,000	2,000	10,000	2,000	200	1,000	200
" " 2 100	1,000	3,000	9,000	3,000	300	900	300
" " 3 100	1,000	4,000	8,000	4,000	400	800	400
" " 4 100	1,000	5,000	7,000	5,000	500	700	500
" " 5 100	1,000	6,000	6,000	6,000	600	600	600
" " 6 100	1,000	7,000	5,000	5,000	700	500	500
" " 7 100	1,000	8,000	4,000	4,000	800	400	400
" " 8 100	1,000	9,000	3,000	3,000	900	300	300
" " 9 100	1,000	10,000	2,000	2,000	1,000	200	200
" " 10 100	1,000	10,000	1,000	1,000	1,000	100	100
1,000	10,000				6,400	5,500	3,500

[Table 6, p. 85, in the original]

Compare depreciation under Ia with depreciation under IIa. In both cases, historical cost is 1,000, while replacement cost increases ten fold. Depreciation based on historical cost (1,000) produces a total of 1,000 units of value, which are calculated as a cost of

100 M. per period at various price levels. No one will dispute that this amount is incorrect in periods of high prices. What must be demonstrated is that the organic depreciation under **IIa** provides enough means to actually acquire a new machine when the old one is retired. This seems impossible since total accumulated depreciation is only 6,400 M., and 10,000 M. are required. The correctness of the idea becomes clear when one recalls that depreciation is very much at one with the organism of the enterprise and continually adapts to the economy along with it. Thus, depreciation at the end of the first year, calculated on the basis of a price level that has doubled, would not be set aside in cash (that would mean removing assets from circulation). Rather, the amount, after being received as proceeds from the sale of merchandise, would immediately appear in a different form on the asset side of the balance sheet since it would be used to acquire new fixed assets or merchandise or to pay wages. It would be simplest to assume, as in the previous example, that new fixed assets were immediately purchased. A newly acquired machine, like all other real assets, would then be subject to the influence of price increases in the following years. Of course one might object that changes in the values of fixed assets do not necessarily move parallel. That only means that it is up to the businessman to acquire assets that hold their value, that is, assets whose value on the average rises at least at the same rate as the general price level. The managerial function of seeking out assets that retain their value is in a poorly developed state today and can only develop fully on the basis of a clear, organic concept of accounting. Nevertheless, we assume its operation in our example. In that case, the value of the asset for which the initial depreciation charge provided the 200 M. purchase price would increase in proportion to the change in the price level over the next nine years, namely to a value of 1,000 M. The same would be true of subsequent depreciation charges, so that the current value of each previous depreciation amount at the end of the tenth year would amount to 1,000 M. Thus, the full amount of the new machine's purchase price would appear in the balance sheet. To be sure, the amount is not cash; in organic accounting, however, it would pose no problem to set aside the cash from the proceeds of current sales. If no opportunities for reinvesting the organic depreciation amount existed, the businessman would receive a capital repayment with the same purchasing power as the corresponding original investment. When the new machine was then acquired at some later date, the businessman would have to withdraw a proportional quantity of purchasing power from the circulation of income.

Technically, the value of depreciation at the time would be credited to a asset replacement account for a total amount of 6,400 M. over ten years. The increase in value would be included in the amount credited from year to year. The entry would include a debit to the capital adjustment account and a credit to the asset replacement account. When an asset was retired, its current value would be removed from the asset replacement account, which would then be cleared of the individual item. Instead of booking the increase in value to the asset replacement account, one could book the entire increase to the capital adjustment account. One would only have to be sure to remove from the capital adjustment account the amount of the new asset's value not included in depreciation, or, in case the depreciation amounts are greater than the new value, to transfer the surplus to capital adjustment. Perhaps it would be easiest to (1) value all fixed assets at current reproduction value as of balance sheet date (reproduction value in unused condition), (2) determine the value of all depreciation charges from previous periods in terms of current reproduction value, and (3) credit the asset replacement account for that amount. The increases in the fixed assets and asset replacement accounts, after the latter is credited with the current year's depreciation amount (dr. profit and loss), are balanced with a credit to the capital adjustment account. The entries would appear as follows:

Fixed Assets Account

Balance from the previous		Ending balance sheet at	
period	100,000	current value	160,000
Addition	30,000		
Capital adjustment account	30,000		

Asset Replacement Account

Ending balance sheet. Current		Depreciation from the previous	
value of depreciation	80,000	period	50,000
		Profit and loss for depreciation	16,000
		Capital adjustment	14,000

Organic accounting proves equally adaptable in all other cases. If **Ib** is compared with **IIa**, the full amount of depreciation (10,000 M. in total) burdens to a disproportionate extent the first years when the value of money is lower. The 1,000 M. invested in real goods in year one are equivalent to 5,000 M. in the last period. The situation is just the opposite if **Ib** and **IIb** are compared when the price level falls sharply and persistently. The depreciation recognized on the value of the asset in the final year of the asset's life (**Ia**, year 10) is definitely not sufficient when the value of the asset is at its highest point.

Indeed, depreciation will have fallen to 100 M. at the end of the asset's depreciable life due to the declining value of the real goods acquired as replacement assets. The initial, organic depreciation of 1,000 M., on the other hand, corresponds exactly to the right amount required to cover the first year's wear and tear. Organic depreciation also proves its merit in the case of varying price movements (IIc). It increases when current replacement value rises and thus permits acquisition of a quantity of goods that actually replaces asset wear and tear. That quantity of goods automatically adapts to all subsequent price changes. The strongest evidence of the correctness of organic depreciation lies in this adaptability, and if the organic concept of accounting proves correct in so important a point, it is difficult to reject it overall.

d) The Valuation of Current Assets

We will consider real current assets first. These include merchandise inventory in the case of a retail enterprise and raw materials in the case of industry. Particularly in the case of industrial production, these real goods, which ultimately are intended for resale, are processed further, that is, charged with costs. But in the retail trade, too, costs are incurred for transportation, storage, packaging, purchasing, and selling in the turnover process. In principle, therefore, there is no difference between retail and industrial enterprises. The only difference lies in the portion of sales price that goes to cover cost of goods sold, and that is only a difference in degree. In either case, operating costs result from input costs plus overhead.

One may well ask the question here: can all these costs be a part of asset valuation in the first place? Both practice and theory have answered in the affirmative as far as real current assets are concerned, that is, in regard to the costs of merchandise inventory and raw materials. Sole proprietors, however, have seldom valued them according to §40 of the Commercial Code, which requires that they be valued as of the date for which inventory and balance sheet are prepared. Rather, they have valued them at lower of cost or market as required for joint-stock companies by §261, 1. §261, 4 expressly forbids manufacturing enterprises operating as joint-stock companies from capitalizing organization and administrative costs. We must take an opposing point of view here. Organization costs become a constituent part of plant assets, and while they are not subject to depreciation, they are subject to changes in value. Thus, they require a return just as much as the costs of acquiring a machine. If we were to disregard this part of the cost of plant assets, it would prevent us from determining the full reproduction value of the enterprise, which is the proper basis for measuring return. Of course, this question relates to the valuation of plant assets.

We are concerned here with current assets and their components, that is, acquisition costs on the one hand and operating and production costs on the other. Production costs have long been included in product cost. We will see that they, like real assets, are subject to changes in value. Our question is how to value current assets and operating costs from a business economics point of view in order to maintain the relative position of the enterprise. Further, is the economy in a position to fulfil these requirements? If a retail enterprise purchased goods at 80, incurred operating costs of 15, and sold the goods at a constant sales price of 100 (leaving a profit of 5), it could only maintain its position in the economy if, at the outset of the next turnover cycle, it could acquire for 80 a quantity of goods of about the same value. That quantity absolutely could be smaller than in the preceding cycle if production decreased or larger if production increased. If inflation causes the price level to rise by 50%, customers will pay 150 for the same quantity of goods. Customers can normally pay this much, and this much must be paid if the economic position of the enterprise is neither to decline nor strengthen. For even if it receives 150 for goods that cost 80 + 15, it now faces acquisition prices and expenses that on the average have risen in proportion to inflation. It will now probably have to pay 120 to acquire goods for resale and 22½ for operating expenses. If it then sells the goods at the same price level, it will realize profit of only 7½, that is, profit in proportion to inflation. And if inflation continues, what at first appears to be profit (and is treated as such today as a result of commingling increases in value with profit) would always be committed immediately to covering the increasing costs of new purchases.

The picture is the same for industrial enterprises that produce goods solely on the basis of labor using no raw materials at all (mining). Individual expenses are incurred at various times within a production cycle. If we abstractly assume (as we have done throughout) that the cost of these expenses remains the same for the current production cycle, it will certainly rise at the beginning of the next one. At the latest, inflation will affect prices at the end of the first cycle, and inflated prices, in turn, will affect depreciation and materials and wages costs incurred in the following cycle. Thus, neither the cost of raw materials nor the cost of labor in the one period can be as high as those in the subsequent, inflated period. They, too, are subject to increases or decreases in value if the price level changes. The question then arises as to the correct value of costs for balance sheet and costing purposes. Assume once again that 95 monetary units were expended throughout the current period for raw materials, wages, and depreciation. Inflation causes the price level to rise by 50%, and customers pay 150 for the goods produced (they pay cash under our assumption). The value of expenses incurred are then measured by the cost to produce approximately the same quantity of goods during the following period. The value for costing purposes is once again replacement value. Replacement value is also the value at which goods still in process at the end of the period should be entered in the balance sheet. We have already demonstrated the necessity of valuing depreciation at replacement cost.

Table 6 shows the accounting treatment of costs and expenses assuming the inflation and varying production of Table 5.

Table 5[*]

Turnover Cycle	Quantity	Costs and Expenses	Revenues	Book Income	Increase (–) or Decrease in Cost of New Production per c	Net Income e – f	Allocation to Reserve (+) or Writeoff from Reserve (–) = g
1	100	95	100	5	-	5	-
2	100	95	150	55	–47½	7½	+47½
3	50	142½	200	57½	–47½	10	+47½
4	10	190	250	60	–47½	12½	+47½
5	50	237½	300	62½	–47½	15	+47½
6	80	285	250	–35	+47½	12½	–47½
7	90	237½	200	–37½	+47½	10	–47½
8	100	190	100	–90	+95	5	–90
9	100	95	100	5	-	5	-
a	b	c	d	e	f	g	h

[*Table 3, p. 54 in the original]

Table 6*¹

Period	Costs and Expenses — 1. Actual costs and expenses	Costs and Expenses — 2. Replacement cost (dr. profit and loss)	Capital Adjustment Account	Capital Adjustment Account	Profit and Loss — 2. Costs and expenses / 4. Net Profit	Profit and Loss — 3. Revenues
1	95	95	—	—	2. Costs and expenses 95 4. Net Profit 5	3. Revenues 100
2	1. " 95 5. Asset valuation 47½	2. do. 142½	—	5. Increase in value (dr.cost and exp.) 47½	2. do. 47½ 4. Net Profit 7½	3. do. 150
3	1. do. 142½ 5. do. 47½	2. do. 190	—	5. do. 47½	2. do. 190 4. do. 10	3. do. 200
4	1. do. 190 5. do. 47½	2. do. 237½	—	5. do. 47½	2. do. 237½ 4. do. 12½	3. do. 250
5	1. do. 237½ 5. do. 47½	2. do. 285	—	5. do. 47½	2. do. 285 4. do. 15	3. do. 300
6	1. do. 285	2. do. 237½ 5. 47½	5. do. 47½	—	2. do. 237½ 4. do. 12½	3. do. 250
7	1. do. 237½	2. do. 190 5. 47½	5. do. 47½	—	2. do. 190 4. do. 10	3. do. 200
8	1. do. 190	2. do. 95 5. 95	5. do. 95	—	2. do. 95 4. do. 5	3. do. 100
9	2. do. 95	2. do. 95	—	—	2. do. 95 4. do. 5	3. do. 100

[*Table 7, p. 91 in the original]

In the first five periods the capital adjustment account is credited 4 times with 47½ monetary units of increased value, all of which disappear again as the price level falls. Indeed, the account would carry a debit balance if the price level continued to fall. The procedure of valuing costs and expenses at replacement cost allows the enterprise to maintain its position from one period to the next whether the price level is rising or falling, in the latter case even when the value of enterprise assets are declining. If we assume that the end of each turnover cycle coincides with the balance sheet date, the value of costs for costing purposes would be the same as those in the balance sheet. If not, the balance sheet values would be replacement values as of the balance sheet date. Of course, these values must always be the *acquisition prices* of raw materials, wages, and fixed asset items; otherwise, future profits are capitalized. The effect of this procedure is to capitalize increases in value, which, however, do not appear as profit on the liabilities side of the balance sheet, but as credits to the capital adjustment account (which is the only correct procedure). In this way, profit is relieved of all changes in value and appears in the profit-and-loss account as genuine profit. The procedure, then, is a practicable way of determining net income during periods of price-level change. Of course, it is the only correct way during periods of stable prices as well.

The value of costs and expenses for costing and balance sheet purposes can differ if the balance sheet date and the end of a turnover cycle do not coincide. In that case, only the value actually on hand as of the balance sheet date can appear in the balance sheet, while cost for costing purposes must be related to the date on which, in the normal course of business, costs are recovered in selling prices.

2. The Valuation of Enterprise Capital

Assume first that an enterprise operates exclusively on equity capital. In that case, the liabilities side of the balance sheet will only contain equity capital. In contrast to today's understanding of the balance sheet, however, equity capital will not remain the same. To be sure, the requirement in §261, 5 that equity capital remain unchanged has only applied to joint-stock companies in the past. In the case of proprietorships and general partnerships, equity capital has increased and decreased because profits were added or deducted that often represented increases or decreases in value.

In organic accounting, equity capital bears all risk. As a part of asset valuation it bears the risk of increases and decreases in value; as a part of income determination, on the other hand, it absorbs all profits (to the extent profits are not distributed or used) and suffers all losses. For the moment we only want to concern ourselves with the effect of changes in asset values on equity capital. When an enterprise is founded, equity capital counterbalances the asset accounts which represent the various assets themselves. The totals on both sides of the balance sheet must be the same. Sometimes (this is true of joint-stock companies), equity capital is divided from the outset into capital stock and reserves. This division has a legal basis, and joint-stock companies must conform to the law. It does not make organic accounting unworkable. We only have to identify the sections into which total equity capital is divided. First, however, we will assume all equity accounts are combined into one.

In that case, equity capital contains the amount of money that corresponds to the current reproduction value of all enterprise assets at the time of its founding. Should the businessman make an especially good buy and acquire the assets below their normal cost, there is an immediate increment in value. An immediate decrease in value is just as possible. The treatment of these decreases in value would be the same as all subsequent decreases in value (which we will deal with first). The monetary values of equity capital and assets are equal at the time the enterprise is founded. This equality can be disturbed if the price-level changes or even if within the same price level shifts in demand occur. A balance sheet date is only a reference point in the periodic determination of the effects of these ever present market forces. Heretofore we have not credited or debited changes in value to equity capital, but to a correction account we have termed "capital adjustment." There can be no question that this account is quite rightly adjunct to equity capital. One could, however, book all changes in value directly to the equity account with equal justification. The effects of price level change on equity are illustrated in Table 7.

As the example indicates:

1. The book value of assets is always equal to the equity capital account plus increases in value or minus decreases in value.

2. Changes in value can be accumulated in a special account to correct for changes in value, or they can be credited or debited to the capital account itself. The latter method

is simpler, but the former permits judgement concerning changes in value since the founding of the enterprise.

Table 7[*]

	Assets side	Liabilities side			Corrected equity capital Account
	Asset values	Equity capital Account	Capital Adjustment (correction for changes in value)		
	Dr.	Cr.	Dr.	Cr.	
Opening balance sheet	1,000	1,000	-	-	1,000
End period 1	2,000	1,000	-	1,000	2,000
" " 2	3,000	1,000	-	2,000	3,000
" " 3	5,000	1,000	-	4,000	5,000
" " 4	10,000	1,000	-	9,000	10,000
" " 5	6,000	1,000	-	5,000	6,000
" " 6	2,000	1,000	-	1,000	2,000
" " 7	1,000	1,000	-	-	1,000
" " 8	500	1,000	500	-	500
" " 9	300	1,000	700	-	300
" " 10	100	1,000	900	-	100
a	b	c	d	e	f

[*Table 8, p. 93 in the original]

3. At the same time, we should note that distributable profit cannot arise from an increment in capital stemming from revaluation of assets. An increase in asset values always counterbalances the increment in capital. Increases in capital due to new contributions of capital may never be credited to the corrections account. Such contributions may only be booked to the capital account or to a reserve account. Only subsequently do changes in the values of assets acquired with the new capital affect the capital adjustment account.

4. Assets are valued at replacement value minus any depreciation, that is, assuming the direct write-off method. If one works with an asset replacement account, assets would be valued at full replacement cost and the replacement account, which would contain the current value of wear and tear, would appear as a contra account on the liabilities side of

the balance sheet.

5. If equity capital is contributed over time at difference price levels, the nominal sum in the capital account commingles unlike amounts, that is, capital of varying strength. The organic balance sheet, however, compensates for these differences by means of the capital adjustment account. The fact that equity capital alone is exposed to the effects of price-level change becomes clear if we assume that in the table above only half of the capital raised when the enterprise was founded is equity capital. The other half is debt capital. Assume further that the value of enterprise assets rises and falls in the same way, as does the capital adjustment account. The basic amount in the capital account, on the other hand, amounts to only 500 units. The other 500 units are in an unvarying liability account. If all changes in value were carried directly to the capital account, the balance in the capital account would always be less than in the preceding example by the 500 units in the liability account.

The fundamental difference between the behavior of equity capital and debt capital under conditions of changing prices becomes quite apparent here. The former bears the full brunt of price-level change, while the latter remains untouched. The differing behaviors give rise to new challenges in structuring the capital of an enterprise that have scarcely been recognized before. We will speak about these challenges under the concept of the equality of values in the balance sheet. Inflation, that is, a rising price level, has a favorable effect on the enterprise and its owners. Not only does the increment in the value of assets acquired with equity capital increase equity capital, but the increment in the value of assets acquired with debt capital does so as well. This development reaches its high point at the end of period 4 in our example. At this point an increase in value of 9,000 units is apportioned to 500 units of equity capital, while debt capital remains fixed at 500 units. The reverse is true when the price level falls. When the price level falls, the total value of assets may fall, as in our example at the end of period 10, to 100 units while debt capital remains on the books at 500 units. As a result of its rigidity, the debt capital pushes the equity capital account onto the asset side of the balance sheet with a loss of 400 units. Practically, the enterprise is overindebted and ripe for bankruptcy from period 9 on. It follows that practice must structure capital so that price-level changes have the best possible effect. This means that during periods of inflation enterprises may work with a large amount of debt capital since by doing so they heighten their prospects of increasing enterprise wealth.   By the same token, if trends reverse, it must strive to convert as much debt capital as possible into equity capital so that decreases in value can be written off of the latter.   In this respect the recent preference for limited-yield preferred stock over industrial bonds is absolutely the correct way of raising new capital assuming inflation is about to come to a halt.   The time to introduce such a financing arrangement is before inflation peaks (an event one always recognizes only after the fact).   This is true because if one is mistaken and inflation continues, the additional increase in prices will affect the values of those assets acquired with equity capital.   In addition, the limited yield on the preferred stock will cause any above normal return that may arise because of continued inflation to be allotted in full to the common shareholders.

Seen in the light of organic accounting, the problem of adapting equity capital to the current price level, especially the equity capital of joint-stock companies, loses its troublesome quality.   Measuring profitability in relation to a fixed capital stock amount that, as is the case today, no longer has anything to do with the intrinsic value of equity capital is meaningless.   Only after adjusting nominal capital for increases or decreases in value does one arrive at the organic balance of equity capital.   If one accepts the essential equivalence of capital stock and corrections for changes in value, the next logical step is to allow joint-stock companies to correct the nominal amount of their share capital.   The company in the example can do so at the end of period 4 by increasing the nominal value of its shares tenfold.   It can accomplish this revaluation by means of overstamping and the entry: dr. asset valuation, cr. capital stock, 9,000.   Of course, proceeding so rapidly is not advisable if one does not expect the price level to hold.   But even if a sharp decline occurred, it would only give rise to the necessity of decreasing the value of share capital again and writing off the decline in value to capital adjustment.   The entry would be: dr. share capital, cr. capital adjustment.

By way of contrast, if one considers today's procedure, which as a matter of law prevents the nominal adjustment of share capital by prohibiting the distribution of bonus shares, a decision in favor of the method described above should not prove difficult. Enterprises today are forced to raise new capital when they do not need it just to conceal from the public such information as the fact that enterprise profits have increased approximately at the same rate as wages. To demand in principle that a new issue of capital stock be sold at market, exploiting in full the current premium, is only justified if the proceeds are to be put to substantive use, not if it is a matter of an issue whose par value is intended to bring total capital in line nominally with its real value.

3. The Equality of Values in the Balance Sheet

Values on both sides of the balance sheet may be divided into those affected by the market and those affected by the value of money, that is, into real items and monetary items. Real items on the asset side of the balance sheet comprise all plant investments on the one hand, including stock held in other companies, and raw materials and work in process on the other. The real item on the liabilities side of the balance sheet - real in the sense of market dependency - is equity capital. The salient feature of real items is that they follow changes in the price level. If the price level rises, their value rises; if it falls, their value falls. On the average, their value rises or falls in proportion to inflation. This is not true, however, of individual assets. The primary task of the businessman is to ensure that the value of every real asset rises or falls at least at the average rate at which prices are changing. He must use his farsightedness to combine to the greatest possible extent those goods that exhibit above normal increases in value or below normal decreases in value. This combination is only achievable if one understands or has a broad view of the market and is conscious of the fact that in the end all values are determined by consumers. The direct influence of consumers is clearly recognizable in the case of inventories. If the businessman anticipates heavy future demand, he will be rewarded with high prices and profits. Errors in this direction result in lower market prices and losses. The stability of enterprise values, however, does not depend on the stability of the value of enterprise products alone, but on overall market conditions as well. A machine in an individual enterprise may manufacture especially high quality products that bring substantial profits. Yet its market value will rise only if increased demand for the machine occurs in all other sectors of the economy. If demand falls in other sectors, the market value of plant assets, materials, labor, etc., also falls.

One should recognize that the businessman has two responsibilities. First, in regard to liquidation, he is to maintain the relative value of the enterprise as measured by the market price of its assets; second, he is to obtain the greatest possible profit from the productive use of those assets.   The former responsibility requires an overview of conditions in the economy as a whole; the latter requires an understanding of the particular market for the specific product.   The incorrect orientation of accounting toward the past has consistently interfered with the first of the two responsibilities.   In general the businessman has not yet become aware of the responsibility.   Only organic asset valuation can sharpen his eye for it.   The most important responsibility will always be to carefully select means of production, to employ them with the greatest possible economy, and to apply them to the production of goods most in demand at the time.

The problem of the equality of values in the balance sheet is a particularly important one at the present time because real and monetary items move in opposite directions.   If the price level rises, real values rise; but the values of cash, receivables, and payables fall accordingly.   Conversely, real items soften if the price level falls, but the value of monetary items firms.   Since the quantities of real and monetary items on the asset and liability sides of the balance sheet may vary considerably, ignoring the opposite effects of price level change may more or less disturb value equilibrium.   Consider the possibilities.

Case A.   Both sides of the balance sheet contain real values only, that is, the liabilities side consists of capital only.   The following balance sheets would result under conditions of stable, increasing, and decreasing values:

I. Stable Values

1.	Plant assets	500	3. Capital	1,000
2.	Inventories	500		

II. Tenfold Increase in Value

1.	Plant assets	5,000	3. Capital	10,000
2.	Inventories	5,000		

III. Tenfold Decrease in Value

1.	Plant assets	50	3. Capital	100
2.	Inventories	50		

Case B. A balance sheet only contains real values on the assets side and monetary values on the liabilities side.

I.

1.	Plant assets	500	3. Debt	1,000
2.	Inventories	500		

II.

1.	Plant assets	5,000	3. Debt	1,000
2.	Inventories representing		4. Increase in value	9,000
	new capital	5,000		

III.

1.	Plant assets	50	3. Debt	1,000
2.	Inventories	50		
4.	Overindebtedness	900		

The debt remains rigidly fixed. When the price level rises, there is an increase in value, which represents new equity capital; when the price level falls, there is a loss in value, which results in overindebtedness. The last case indicates the risk involved in acquiring real assets with debt capital. A decline in the price level leaves the debt intact at its original amount, but causes a decline in the value of the counterbalancing assets so that overindebtedness and collapse become inevitable. Conversely, when the price level rises, the entire increase in asset values represents new equity capital. Thus, the businessman should strive to work with as much debt capital as possible when the price level is rising and with as little as possible when the price level is falling. The question remains as to how one can structure capital so that one is always safe. Since no one can have certain knowledge of future price-level developments, the only sure way to proceed is to acquire all real assets with equity capital and to finance all cash and receivables by incurring debt.

The balance sheets in the above cases would then appear as follows:

I.

1.	Plant assets	500	5. Equity capital	750
2.	Inventories	250	6. Debt	250
3.	Receivables	200		
4.	Cash reserves for production	50		

II.

1.	Plant assets	5,000	5. Equity capital	7,500
2.	Inventories	2,500	6. Debt	250
3.	Receivables	200		
4.	Cash reserves for production	50		

III.

1.	Plant assets	50	5. Equity capital	75
2.	Inventories	25	6. Debt	250
3.	Receivables	200		
4.	Cash reserves for production	50		

Value equilibrium would be disturbed if, say, the 250 units of debt balanced real goods or the 250 units of monetary assets balanced equity capital. When the price level clearly moves in a certain direction, the businessman can benefit from a disproportionate capital structure. In times of uncertainty about price-level developments, it is to his benefit to choose value equilibrium. Incidentally, the example does not indicate another benefit of the free economic play of organic accounting. If one consciously chooses to structure real and monetary values on an equilibrium basis, the values will maintain their proportionality as the turnover process takes place, that is, if the price level falls, the amount of debt in the economy as a whole shows a tendency to fall, and vice versa. This becomes clear if one considers on what monetary assets depend. The items in question include production and credit funds. Their amount likewise depends on the price level. In total the funds may normally amount to 250 units, of which 50 represent a cash reserve for wages and other costs, while the remaining 200 represent credit items, that is, trade accounts receivable. The 250 units of monetary value would also rise or fall with the price level. The following observations will illustrate this.

If when prices are stable organic accounting values all cost components at the replacement value of goods sold, one would normally need 250 units to finance current monetary requirements. That amount is borrowed. If then the price level fell to one tenth, the value of inventory would fall as well, as would the amount of credit extended, so that one would be in a position to repay 225 units. Conversely, if the price level rose tenfold, the need for debt would increase ten times. The increased need for debt, however, would be covered with no special difficulty from national income, which will have increased proportionately.

What follows from these relationships is the primary dictum of the equality of values in the balance sheet, that is, that the businessman should always strive to achieve harmony in the valuation process relative to both debt and equity if the enterprise is to remain secure during periods of price-level change.

If equality of values is maintained, the problem of liquidity is limited to harmoniously timing the maturity dates of monetary values on both sides of the balance sheet. One must always be in a position to liquidate more assets than payables currently due. If that is the case, the enterprise is absolutely safe as long as receivables are not dishonored, that is, debtors do not fail to repay debts on demand. Reserves should be formed to cover such losses, allocations to which should be made from current profits. With regard to the question of measuring rate of return, asset valuation provides part of the basis, namely the total value of the assets currently on hand, measured in terms of the price level that prevails in the economy. Exact determination of operating profit is then required to relate income to the value of assets, that is, to calculate rate of return. That ratio, in turn, indicates how successful the businessman has been in utilizing the goods and economic forces that constitute his enterprise more economically than the marginal producer. At least a normal rate of return means enterprise assets are being preserved; a below normal rate of return means enterprise assets are being dissipated; an above normal return means assets are being increased as long as the above normal profit is not distributed.

D. Organic Income Calculation[*]

Fritz Schmidt

a) Basic Principles

Enterprise net income is what is left of sales after all replacement costs of production have been recovered. One can speak of income in terms of organic accounting only if enterprise sales at least allow the enterprise to maintain its productive capacity relative to that of the economy as a whole. This basic principle represents the cornerstone of our study. The function of income calculation, accordingly, is above all the determination of economically correct costs from this point of view. The basic question in this respect is the valuation of costs. Traditional, statistical costing depends on actual, historical expenditures. Depreciation, wages, and raw materials are recorded in accordance with actual amounts paid. The procedure is safe and yields the same results as organic accounting if no price-level changes occur between date of original purchase and cost recovery at point of sale. It becomes folly if price-level changes do occur; folly because the purchase of a machine or raw materials in the past says nothing about cost of replacement and because yesterday's wages are no measure of what they will be during the next pay period. The organic approach to cost proceeds from the principle of the maintenance of the relative value of the enterprise; maintenance of relative value we say because as our introductory observations indicated [i.e., in the introductory chapters] the natural tendency of a free economy during periods of price-level change is to maintain the productive capacity of an enterprise whose significance for satisfying demand remains the same. Maintenance of relative value because it depends on the relationship between national income on the one hand and available goods on the other. If the relationship shifts unilaterally - if income rises or falls while the availability of goods remains the same -, proportionately higher or lower costs are assigned to goods; if the availability of goods changes, the same costs are assigned to more or fewer goods. In the latter case in particular this means that the manufacturer may only recover the replacement cost of goods and services truly necessary

---

[*]   Extract from Fritz Schmidt, *Die organische Bilanz im Rahmen der Wirtschaft*, 1921, pp. 100-119.

for the ensuing cycle but not depreciation, materials, or wages not required for the particular volume of production. Excess plant and equipment and surplus raw materials then become subject to declines in value. Such assets that are no longer part and parcel of production should be segregated, and if the situation appears to be permanent, sold to other producers or consumers who are able to put them to greater use and thus pay reasonable prices for them.

What is important then is above all clarification of the replacement cost principle.

If we consider enterprise, balance sheet, and income calculation more closely, we can distinguish two spheres: (1) the turnover sphere [*Umsatzsphäre*] and (2) the monetary sphere [*Geldsphäre*]. The principle of cost accumulation and sale at actual cost (= historical cost) places all price changes in the monetary sphere; that is, if all the costs contained in sales price are not sufficient to maintain relative production, the additional demand for capital must be satisfied by raising new capital, whether in the form of debt capital or equity capital. If prices fall, repayment of capital proportional to the excess of cost recovered over replacement cost is the result. This method leads to enterprise impoverishment during periods of inflation and to enterprise enrichment during periods of deflation. It is the method of the past, and its ruinous effect today is cause enough to reject it.

Costing on the basis of cost on cost date, that is, on the day the cost component is consumed,[1] improves matters to some extent. It places changes in values that occur between acquisition and use in production in the turnover sphere, but others, those that occur from use in production to sale or replacement, in the monetary sphere. Increases in the prices of cost components after cost date must then be covered using new capital during the ensuing cost cycle; decreases, counterbalanced by capital repayments. In either case the relationship between debt and equity changes.

Within the framework of the replacement cost principle, several possibilities exist for demarcating the turnover and monetary spheres. The latter sphere comprises in addition to

---

[1] Cf. Schmalenbach's article on cost valuation ("Selbstkostenrechnung," *Zeitschrift für handelswissenschaftliche Forschung*, 1919, p. 274ff.) Schmalenbach would record cost at market value on the date the order is placed and the parties agree on price (p. 283). He also recommends adjusting the value of inventories subsequently. But then he cannot avoid the fact that revenues impair productive capacity when prices are rising and enhance it when prices are falling.

cash balances all monetary receivables and payables necessary for production; the former, all real goods, whether plant and equipment or current assets and services. The boundary between the two spheres shifts according to the point in time to which we relate cost. If we use actual replacement cost - and it makes no difference how far in the future payment is postponed by using credit -, all cash balances and monetary receivables become part of the turnover sphere, that is, if income levels rise, sales revenue must be great enough to include the surcharges necessary to cover full replacement cost on actual date of replacement as compared to replacement cost on date of sale. The turnover sphere, as the domain of equity capital, assimilates all increases and decreases in value. We saw in the discussion of the equality of values in the balance sheet that during periods of inflation equity capital absorbs all increases in value and that during periods of deflation it absorbs all decreases in value (which could deplete it if developments were precipitous enough), while debt capital remained rigid and fixed. One could only avoid overindebtedness by converting debt capital into equity capital. Such disharmony in adapting to the situation leads one to wonder whether or not a compromise is possible that will overcome it.

Much speaks in favor of assuming that a proportional structuring of the turnover sphere (= equity capital) and the monetary sphere (= debt capital) is possible if one relates the replacement cost principle to "cost to replace as of day of sale" (the day the concrete product becomes money or a receivable), that is, if one uses replacement cost as of the day the finished good changes hands on the market. That day is the day of sale only if it occurs after the good itself is finished, not when merely ordered since many cost components are consumed only after order date. It is the day of delivery only when ordered in advance and not when finished goods are sold with a provision for subsequent delivery. This date will henceforth be termed day of market transfer, turnover date, or day on which both production and sale are complete. From a business economics point of view, the significance of this definition is that at the beginning of each production cycle the turnover and monetary spheres overlap. As we have already seen, revenues from cash sales can only be used in part for immediate replacement of cost components. To the extent immediate replacement is possible, money merely represents a general warrant for goods. In principle, then, one assures the continuity of production by replacing cost components at the moment of sale, that is, by replacing them at the same price level at which the product is sold. This procedure is possible for materials and plant, although in the case of plant not in the sense that consumption of one tenth of a machine's useful life in one period will purchase one tenth of a new machine in the next. Rather, a machine that happens to need replacing can be acquired from the one-tenth consumption of all machines in use. To the extent that no replacement is possible because no plant is retired, a corresponding portion of equity capital may be liquidated.

Other cost components, particularly wages, light, power, heat, etc., do not turn over continually, that is, they are not immediately replaceable at the close of a production cycle. Their replacement cost must remain in the form of money until in the course of the new cycle wages, light, power are used and paid for. If we figure sales price using replacement cost as of day of sale, that portion of revenue that cannot be used immediately to replace cost components moves from the turnover sphere (which automatically follows the movement of the price level) into the rigid and nominally fixed monetary sphere. On the one hand, the result is the possibility that wage levels will rise leaving the amount reserved for replacement insufficient to continue production at the same level; and on the other that if wage levels fall the total amount will not be used. If replacement amounts are not sufficient, new debt must be incurred; if there is an excess amount, debt can be retired. Whenever the value of turnover capital changes, monetary capital changes quantitatively.

It would appear, therefore, that we have found the natural boundary between equity capital and debt capital by calculating cost on the basis of replacement value on day of sale. It appears natural, and thus correct, because costing on this basis solves the problem of changing prices and preserves the relative position of the enterprise as well as the relationship between equity and debt. Let's start with the last example in the section on the equality of values in the balance sheet. The example involved the following opening balance sheet, which should be understood as coincident with the beginning of a new production cycle.

1.	Plant and Equipment	500	5.	Equity	750
2.	Materials for the next		6.	Debt	250
	production cycle	250			
3.	Accounts receivable	200			
4.	Cash reserves for production	50			

To the extent the price level rises or falls during the new production cycle the value of real assets and equity capital rises and falls in complete harmony. Monetary value *quantity* moves in a similar manner on both the debit side (3 and 4) and the credit side (6). This means that if the prices of goods and wages are rising, increased amounts of money become necessary for payment of accounts payable and wages, and if the increased amounts are not available, they must be financed by incurring additional debt. If the price level falls, replacement costs and receipts from receivables in subsequent periods are not required in full, and debt can be reduced proportionately.

A permanently proportional arrangement in the balance sheet depends on the date one chooses to value replacement costs. If one chooses actual replacement cost (for periodic costs as well as immediately replaceable costs), monetary values move from the monetary sphere into the turnover sphere, with the result that debt becomes rigidly fixed while the value of equity rises or falls faster than the price level. The danger is that if the price level falls precipitously, the enterprise will become overindebted. Use of historical cost means that real values slip from the turnover sphere into the monetary sphere and that equity becomes fixed, that is, that equity does not increase or decrease as the price level rises or falls. This is true because sales revenue only covers historical costs, and increases in prices have to be met by raising additional (initially debt) capital and decreases in prices by liquidating capital. The new capital would rise or fall out of proportion. Thus, only use of replacement cost as of the day of market transfer remains as the middle ground that maintains equity and debt capital in the same proportion and affects equity and debt in proportion to changes in the price level. It is the only valuation method that allows the enterprise to adapt harmoniously to business cycles, and for this reason it must form the basis for income calculation.

The harmony required by business economics also finds support from an economy-wide point of view. If one uses historical cost (which has been the custom to date), then when prices are rising one sells goods below the value assigned them by the last customer willing to purchase them, and income normally devoted to consumer goods remains free for investment. Thus, the relationship between consumption and investment undergoes artificial modification economy-wide much as occurred under the pressure of price controls during the war. Old enterprise owners become relatively dispossessed. New groups of investors who assign costs more nearly correctly or at least obtain market prices (dealers and black marketeers) become owners of production facilities. Enterprise equity no longer is sufficient to maintain normal production if only monetary items are increased proportionately. New capital must be raised from the funds made available by the shift from consumption to investment. If the price level falls, costing at historical cost causes equity to increase disproportionately and more income to be spent on consumption so that enterprises need no new capital at all. Instead, they tend to liquidate capital since replacement of cost components does not require full use of that portion of sales revenue representing cost recovery. The capital so liquidated, in turn, reinforces consumption. We know, of course, that market forces resist such developments, but the orientation of our entire national economic policy and all our businessmen toward an incorrect cost value exerts considerable influence.

If costs of total production were based on actual replacement cost, one would, under conditions of inflation, have to charge a price that at the moment of sale contained a greater cost-of-wages quota than warranted by wage levels as of the day of sale. The wage earner would receive fewer goods than he produced. Under conditions of deflation, on the other hand, the wage earner could purchase more than he produced with his current income if sales price on day of sale contained a lower cost-of-wages quota relating to the future. During inflation all increases in value would increase equity. National income would increase out of proportion to consumption and decrease out of proportion to investment. Just the opposite is true if prices are falling.

A proportional structuring of the consumption and investment components of the national income becomes possible only if costs of production are based on replacement cost as of day of sale. If costs are based on replacement cost as of day of sale, the wage earner pays a price containing a cost-of-wages component at the same level as his own current one; and if that equality is the case, the relative value of an enterprise's equity capital and the relative quantity of its debt capital remain proportional just as do those components of the national income attributable to consumption and investment if income merely increases or decreases.

Recognition of the fundamental difference between the turnover and monetary spheres at the enterprise level also finds support at the national level. Items in the turnover sphere are real items and thus constitute national wealth; items in the monetary sphere on the other hand are monetary items - cash holdings, receivables, and payables - that arise from the circulation of the national income. Cash holdings can only be considered a part of national wealth when they are set aside for the purchase of goods. Receivables and payables represent, respectively, reserved income and income expended in advance. Since every receivable necessarily entails a corresponding debt, the two sides offset one another and thus cannot constitute a part of national wealth.

I can assert one thing here without further study, that is, that an increase or decrease in national income is not without influence on the nominal amount of that portion of income intended for investment on the one hand and savings on the other. The increase in bank deposits and stock issuances in the past few years reflects this influence. I am not saying that the relationship between income invested and income saved should always remain proportional. That would require closer study. But that the investment portion does not increase alone as a result of the workings of the market under inflationary conditions (and when cost is based on actual replacement cost) is just as certain as the impossibility of a unilateral increase in savings as a result of costing on the basis of historical cost. For this reason, costing on the basis of replacement cost as of day of sale best meets the demands of the economy as a whole. It does so because it adjusts the values in the turnover sphere and the monetary sphere proportionately and thus adapts most reliably to the natural allocation of income. There is no reason to believe that either the urge to invest or the urge to save might increase unilaterally. After all, the need to save is to a large extent the result of periodic income payments to salaried workers and seasonal entrepreneurs, both of whom gradually use income after receiving and depositing it in lump sums. As income levels rise, the amount saved automatically rises as well.

But in the case of a general shift in production, too, replacement cost as of day of sale is the cost value that guarantees complete harmony of the economy. Assume income remains the same and production falls so that only half the goods are produced in the current period as were produced previously. At the close of the previous period (the last period that produced a full supply of goods) costing goods sold at replacement cost as of day of sale provides sufficient means to completely replace plant wear and tear as well as materials (only half of the previous quantity being required). The cost of wages, which increases as a result of the fall in production, can also be met because at most, as long as the national income remains the same, it can only double. Thus, in total it cannot amount to more than the replacement cost of wages for the period preceding the decline in production provided labor output remains the same.

At the end of the period in which production declines, replacement cost on day of sale easily covers reduced plant wear and tear, the reduced quantity of materials required, and wages which have remained the same or fallen. To the extent that wages and prices adapt slowly because of technical constraints, a portion of the replacement cost remains unused. That portion serves to liquidate capital and, as increased purchasing power when investment opportunities are limited, probably accelerates inflationary tendencies and thus the adjustment to new conditions.

One can picture the situation most clearly if one imagines the decline in production taking place period by period and in jolts. In that case, period one sets a full measure of production opposite a full measure of national income; period two, on the other hand, a half measure of production with a full measure of national income. Prices and wages per unit of product remain constant throughout period one. At the beginning of period two, they double. Plant consumption is recovered in full at a one-fold cost from period one's production; materials and wages in period two at half their quantity or intensity, but at twice their cost. At the end of period two, replacement cost as of day of sale permits complete replacement of reduced plant consumption and of materials and labor at double their cost or, if the production decline continues, for the latter two factors at an even higher amount for even less quantity or intensity. The relationship between equity capital and debt capital remains nominally unaffected as long as, say, the relationship between demand for plant and demand for labor does not shift for technical reasons. Of course, a different quantity of real values stands opposite the nominally proportional equity and debt capital. Only plant actually used in production retains its value; the remainder loses value for the moment, although its value may be restored in the future when the plant in use is fully consumed. Quantitatively, goods produced for sale will also have fallen by one half.

If production increases, the picture is just the opposite. Materials are less expensive and wages are lower or more productive during period two. At the end of the period, more plant consumption and more materials and labor can be recouped. To the extent the increase in production occurs with greater plant consumption or more intense use of plant, the relationship between equity and debt capital does not change. The demand for additional plant and equipment can only be met gradually.

The principle of costing at replacement cost as of day of sale also operates harmoniously in cases of specific production changes. These changes can be attributed to shifts in demand. If we assume that national income remains the same, it means that the demand for the goods of a production facility rises or falls because consumers have changed their minds about the utility of the goods. But the costs of production - plant consumption, wages, materials, etc. - have not changed. Under these conditions, the quantity of goods that can be sold above cost decreases or increases. If it decreases, the consumer only allows recovery of the actual costs of cost components, that is, in full in the period prior to the decline in production, but to a lesser extent in the following period. The businessman will then either have to dismiss workers and close plants or manufacture a new product. In the former case, he can reduce capital nearly proportionately by using proceeds from the sale of excess plant and raw materials, wage reserves that are no longer necessary, and amounts no longer required for trade credits. In the case of specific increases in production, the necessary increases in plant, materials, and labor must be funded with new capital. Raising new capital is made easier by the fact that every specific increase in production is accompanied by a specific decline in production elsewhere in the economy that makes available plant, materials, workers, and capital.

From an organic point of view, the proper value for costing purposes is replacement cost as of date of market transfer. Costing on this basis, every enterprise will be able to maintain its relative position in the economy, if, that is, it operates at least at normal efficiency. Practically, this means that the enterprise should recover from the sales price of its products a sufficient quantity of money to acquire, given a proportional increase in debt during the following production period, a more or less equivalent quantity of plant, materials, and labor. During inflation, it is the same quantity; if production declines, a relatively smaller quantity; if production increases, a relatively greater quantity. To be sure, one should not overlook the fact that in the latter two cases a shift in production also occasions a shift in the point of maximum return, which may result in businesss closings on the one hand and the creation of enterprises on the other.

Of special importance is that what business economics requires be in strict harmony with what the national economy permits. If personal income rises, the economy as a whole can pay higher replacement values. It is able to do so on the strength of the laws of the market, which, by the same token, force the purchase of less if personal incomes fall. If production declines, it is true that more can be paid per unit of product as long as national income remains the same; but fewer goods can be produced in the following period if the cost of plant, materials, and wages have risen. Increases in production have the opposite effect. One could formulate these relationships as follows, although the result may prove impracticable. In the case of shifts in production with no change in national income, the economy can only pay the same total costs during any turnover cycle. In a period of declining productivity, the total cost is spread over fewer goods; in a period of increasing productivity, it is spread over more goods and their costs. Individual cost components should not be thought of as exactly proportional if technical or social influences cause the shift in productivity. Indeed, a reallocation of capital and labor may become necessary. When income undergoes inflation, on the other hand, market prices also become inflated, and the replacement values of costs rise proportionately.

The above discussion by no means exhausts the matter, but it does identify its most important points. Until now we have concentrated primarily on enterprises with a normal return. Factories with above normal profits are those that are better able to exploit cost outlays. Because they are more efficient, they produce more goods from the same plant facilities, materials, and labor, and thus realize a greater return. Those that earn a below normal return deplete assets since they realize so little revenue they are unable to cover replacement costs. The disparity here attests to the wide latitude the businessman enjoys in striving for the highest possible return at the lowest possible cost. He must constantly be alert that the mix of assets making up his enterprise yields at least a normal return, and he must always strive to employ his assets in the most profitable manner possible. He must manufacture those products most highly prized and sought after by consumers. He can only do so, however, if accounting provides him with reliable and unequivocal standards of measure. Present methods simply do not offer such measures.

If we establish the principle that cost must equal replacement cost on date of market transfer (the organic view), we incorporate a future value into our calculation. That value can only be determined with absolute certainty if we calculate cost on day of sale. Determination of such costs is particularly difficult for enterprises that receive orders on the basis of firm bids and only begin production after concluding an agreement. Today one sees protective measures being taken instinctively against the risks of such advance cost calculations in subject-to clauses, in provisos allowing price increments in case of price-level change, and in advance payments. As a matter of fact, these measures represent organic solutions to the problem. If one calculates cost as of date of tender, replacement cost on day of market transfer can only be realized if all price-level changes up to the date the goods become ready for delivery are incorporated in price. Of course a price reduction is also in order if replacement costs fall. Costing at replacement cost is easiest when goods are sold promptly and immediate replacement is possible.

It is true that covering future replacement costs in this way introduces an element of uncertainty and occasions a kind of currency speculation, but one will surely prefer this accounting if one is convinced that traditional historical cost accounting gives rise to incorrect profit-or-loss figures. Besides, my earlier observations concerning the equality of values in the balance sheet indicated that it is possible to influence replacement date, that is, to more nearly equate it with the present by paying in advance. One can see this possibility most clearly in the retail trade in which lengthy production processes do not disrupt turnover cycles. Assume the price of a good is 10 monetary units in cycle one, 20 in cycle two, and 30 in cycle three. The replacement cost of the good at the outset of cycle two will be 20 monetary units in place of the ten originally paid. The sales price should incorporate the increase in cost along with all the other costs. But if the good were purchased in advance during cycle one, ten monetary units would suffice for replacement, provided, of course, that immediate replacement were technically possible. The situation would be just the opposite if prices were falling, that is, if replacement cost were 30 monetary units in the present cycle and 20 in the following. Under these conditions, prepayment would amount to 30 monetary units. No one would pay in advance since future cash value would only amount to 20 monetary units. The whole affair clearly explains why under conditions of rising prices - such as prevail today - replacements are paid for in cash and in advance, but any reverse in trends brings immediate offers of deferred payment pending delivery. In the industrial sector determination of replacement value is somewhat more difficult since bids are frequently made on the basis of calculated prices whose actual costs lie in the future as well as their replacement costs.

Cost accumulation as we have described it here unfortunately cannot be expressed with any precision in monetary units of the present. Rather, it is primarily a matter of the right attitude on the part of the businessman toward future transactions, which always entail speculation. If a businessman sells goods under conditions of changing prices, he engages in speculation. The organic point of view at least allows the businessman insight into how to adapt, how to adjust his prices. In doing so he must always remain clearly aware of the difference between shifts in income levels and shifts in production. If the former alone occurs, future replacement values and the prices of individual goods generally rise or fall in proportion to the shift in income. In the case of shifts in production, replacement values and the prices of individual goods also rise or fall, but replacement values do not rise or fall completely proportionately because in the following period production must expand or contract to maintain the relative position of the enterprise. In either case, calculation of cost prior to sale, which at best only incorporates actual costs, cannot serve as the sole basis for setting price. The businessman must seek the highest price possible in the market. That price may well cover replacement cost since sales prices would derive from the same price level at which replacement costs are to be valued. To the extent immediate replacement is not possible, the price level on replacement date permits the necessary corrections to replacement value for changes in the value of money. After-the-fact calculation of historical cost, then, allows determination of actual replacement costs.

The problems of day-to-day price setting are less critical in the framework of income determination. While the replacement value of cost components is often uncertain at the moment of sale, it is usually an historical figure for purposes of calculating book income, or if not, a currently available one. To be sure, one usually charges the profit-and-loss account with the actual costs of individual expense items on a current basis. One books materials used at historical cost; wages and salaries, etc., at the amount of cash paid. Organic accounting incorporates replacement values by booking the difference between actual cost and replacement cost as exactly what it is, that is, as an increase or decrease in the value of enterprise assets. That such changes in value occur is unavoidable and have already been treated in the chapter on accounting for assets. On the whole, accounting for assets properly is not particularly difficult.

As long as price-level changes are due solely to changes in national income with no accompanying shifts in productivity, an enterprise has, according to the principle of the maintenance of relative value, every right to continue the same level of production after each replacement cycle. The replacement values of all the costs of a particular cycle, therefore, are determined by their cost at the close of the cycle. Their value, accordingly, is market value on day of sale. Practically, this means that if a retail enterprise has an average cash-to-cash cycle of, say, three months and if the costs of the four cycles for the current year are as shown in the following table [Table 8], the replacement costs for Cycle I are the same as the actual costs of Cycle II, to the extent, that is, replacement takes place immediately after sale. Otherwise, they must be valued severally by cost on day of sale. Under this assumption one could determine the increase or decrease in costs for Cycle I so as to compare the actual costs of Cycle I with the actual costs of Cycle II. If there is an increase for Cycle II, the increase represents the increase in costs during Cycle I. If, on the other hand, the value for Cycle I is greater than that of Cycle II, the difference represents a decline in the value of cost items as a result of a change in national income and not a loss as traditional accounting would say. The following example will clarify the matter.

Table 8[*]

Turnover cycle (3 months)	Costs for the cycle	Sales revenue	Replacement costs at the beginning of the next cycle	Change in the value of costs	Profit
I	1,000	2,200	2,000	1,000	200
II	2,000	3,300	3,000	1,000	300
III	3,000	4,400	4,000	1,000	400
IV	4,000	5,500	5,000	1,000	500
V	(5,000)	(6,600)	-	-	-
	10,000 (15,000)	15,400 (22,000)	14,000	4,000	1,400
a	b	c	d	e	f

[*Table 9, p. 114 in the original]

The following observations might be made regarding the numbers: the historical costs of the production cycle appear in column **b**. The figures given for wages and salaries, which timewise are very closely tied to the turnover process, represent actual cash payments, as do those for a few other costs such as for power, light, and heat. Actual expenditures for cost components whose acquisition may occur before the production cycle normally requires, on the other hand, (such timing depending on the disposition of the businessman) may vary. This is especially true for raw materials, which in some circumstances may be purchased on credit quite some time before their use. Costing in this manner only means that increases or decreases in value will appear in the raw materials accounts.

The cost of depreciation should be entered as the replacement cost of plant consumed as of the end of the production cycle. For Cycle I it would be the fixed assets consumed during that period of time. But even here it is only a matter of dividing the change in value into two parts. If, for example, a fixed asset that was being depreciated at a rate of 10% per cycle had been purchased for 10,000 M. and its replacement cost at the beginning of Cycle I were 30,000 M. and at the end of Cycle I 60,000 M., the replacement cost for Cycle I would be 60,000 M. and the cost of depreciation 6,000 M. This cost would have to be booked as the replacement cost for Cycle I. The difference between historical cost (10,000) and the replacement cost for the cycle (60,000) = 50,000 M. less depreciation to date (for approximately five cycles at 10% = 30,000, minus depreciation calculated on the basis of historical cost = 5,000) would then be recorded in the asset valuation account. The increase in value for the asset in question, therefore, is 30,000 − 5,000 = 25,000. The calculation of replacement cost depreciation would be easiest if one first debited the profit-and-loss account for book-value depreciation. The book value of fixed assets could be historical cost if one did not stop there but calculated changes in value separately. Or it could be replacement cost at the end of the preceding cycle if one periodically increased the individual assets to their end-of-cycle replacement value in the accounts. In that case the difference between end-of-cycle replacement value and replacement value on day of sale would have to be charged subsequently to the profit-and-loss account. If, however, as is usually the case, the income period encompasses several turnover cycles, one should use mean replacement values for cost components; for revenues may stem from widely differing price levels and may only be matched with replacement costs of current delivery dates in any case. Of course the relevant replacement cost for an incomplete cycle at fiscal year-end still lies in the future. Practically, however, the cycle usually comes to an end before the year-end accounting work is done. In the case of continual turnover or continuous production with little variation in output, one may use mean values for the year if the change in prices takes place evenly. Otherwise one should compute an average based on turnover volume and replacement price. Computation of mean replacement values is not necessary if the price level remains constant. As for the rest, one has to content oneself with approximations. Even if there are no other uncertainties, estimating the useful life of a fixed asset has always been a difficult task. In any event, knowledge of the right principle brings us much nearer the truth than otherwise would be possible.

Column c of Table 8 contains sales amounts. Our earlier discussion concerning the effects of inflation explained why revenues necessarily move parallel to historical costs as well as replacement costs. Profit, which actually depends on enterprise economy, was assumed to be 10% of current replacement cost. It cannot fall below zero for long; if so, one soon begins to deplete assets, including cost components whose cost is not recovered in sales revenue. There is every reason to believe that dissipation of cost components has already begun if at least (1) a normal rate of return on enterprise capital and (2) entrepreneurial compensation are not earned.

Column d contains the replacement costs of each cycle. I have already covered the essentials here. In principle, the numbers represent cost at the moment of market transfer. If replacement takes place over the entire cycle, the proportional effect of inflation on enterprise liabilities compensates for subsequent price changes.

Column e shows the changes in the values of cost components. The changes in value arise because cost components are affected by price-level changes that occur between point of use in production or (and this may be applicable) point of acquisition and market transfer. Accounting heretofore has included these changes in enterprise profit. During periods of price-level stability, it is a matter of ups and downs in the economy. During periods of inflation, on the other hand, it becomes a matter of isolating the effect of price-level change on the value of enterprise assets. The value of enterprise assets, however, is not only a matter of fixed assets and materials, but of wages and salaries as well, which are equally subject to the effects of price-level change.

Column **f**, finally, shows net income as determined according to organic principles, that is, net of all changes in the value of enterprise assets. Calculated in this manner, its magnitude depends exclusively on internal enterprise economy. It signifies the extent to which the enterprise has succeeded in producing at a lower cost than other enterprises of the same kind, especially the least profitable enterprise whose existence is necessary to satisfy demand.

b) Organic Income Determination

In order to demonstrate the calculation of book income in the manner suggested by the table in the preceding section (Table 8, p. 182), we need to dispense with all the details that might otherwise obscure the important points. Assume therefore that the various revenues and expenses that would otherwise be distributed among several accounts (wages, interest, raw materials, inventory, etc.) are debited or credited directly to the profit-and-loss account. That account would then contain the amounts in columns **b** and **c** at year-end, namely historical costs and sales. As explained above in the discussion of **b**, costs do not always have to be correct timewise. Since replacement value corrects for time, it makes no difference if one initially uses historical costs for materials and depreciation.

The various costs that in practice would first be debited to separate expense accounts such as materials, wages, salaries, light, power, etc., appear under **1** of Table 9 below. The amounts also contain depreciation, which may be construed as based on historical cost or replacement value as of day of sale. In the former case, it would be relatively low under conditions of inflation. The traditional method of calculating income would then compare total sales (**2** of Table 9), which would also initially appear in various individual accounts (merchandise inventory, finished goods, sales), with expenses and record profit for the year at 5,400 units. According to organic principles, on the other hand, increases in the value of cost components that have occurred between acquisition date (or date of use in production) and day of sale must be isolated and debited to the capital adjustment account. The amount is found by comparing the costs debited to date with their replacement value on day of market transfer. The method yields an exact measure of replacement cost that reflects reality and that provides a sound footing in case of dispute. Replacement value exceeds historical cost for each cycle by 1,000 units. These 4,000 units of extra cost are not profit according to the organic viewpoint. They cannot be because their distribution would render impossible the maintenance of enterprise value. They represent increases in the value of cost components, of enterprise assets. Only if an additional charge for these extra costs is made to the profit-and-loss account can actual profit be calculated, which in this case appears as 1,400 units. Actual replacement costs of the replacement cycle, however, can be greater than historical cost plus the increase in

Table 9[*]

Profit-and-Loss Account

Dr. (Expenses)			Cr. (Revenues)		
1. Historical costs			2. Sales		
	Period I	1,000		Period 1	2,200
	Period II	2,000		Period II	3,300
	Period III	3,000		Period III	4,400
	Period IV	4,000		Period IV	5,500
		10,000			
3. Changes in value of costs in each cycle as measured by replacement costs (cr. capital adjustment account) on day of sale		4,000			
4. Enterprise net profit		1,400			
		15,400			15,400

[*Table 10, p. 117 in the original]

value to day of sale since not all costs that are recovered, such as wages, salaries, light, can be replaced on day of sale. Increases in the value of these items, which must be paid for out of production reserves, must be offset by incurring debt and decreases in value by repaying debt.

The example deals with inflationary price increases which are topical at the moment. The time is probably not far away when the majority of prices, which are already vacillating, will show a tendency to fall.

Of course, we will never achieve the old price level. When prices do fall, the historical cost amount that appears on the expense side will be greater than replacement cost. As a result, there would be a corresponding credit to the capital adjustment account for the decline in value; otherwise enterprises are likely to report losses that are in fact declines in value - declines in value which every other citizen would have to suffer without being excused from the payment of an income tax. A summary example follows:

Profit-and-Loss Account

1.	Total historical costs for the fiscal year	18,000	2. Sales for the fiscal year	15,400
4.	Enterprise net profit	1,400	3. Decline in value credited to the capital adjustment account	4,000
		19,400		19,400

It is not necessary to discuss the matter of profit further here. The rules of traditional practice remain valid in all other respects. Organic profit as genuine surplus can be distributed in full without compromising the relative position of the enterprise within the ranks of its competitors. Organic profit alone is genuine income. As such, it is an amount that ought to be of keen interest the tax authorities. If such profit is retained in the firm in part or in total, it will for the most part enter production during the next production cycle and become a component of enterprise assets. It will then appear on the debit side of the balance sheet as a fixed or current asset and on the credit side as an increase in the equity account or a special (reserve) account.

Organic profit is net profit on turnover and thus realized profit. It results from costing on the basis of replacement cost. Replacement cost is always current cost plus incidental costs to acquire. If costs are valued accordingly and total costs compared with sales, the result is net turnover profit. Turnover is a precondition of completing a production cycle via sale. If a cycle is not complete, that is, if inventory is still on hand at fiscal year-end, there is no related profit. Inventories are entered in the balance sheet at year-end replacement cost, which may result in increases or decreases in asset values vis-à-vis historical cost. Thus, balance sheet replacement cost is not the same as replacement cost for costing purposes: the two values differ as a matter of timing. Attempting to use the latter value for unsold inventories (replacement cost for costing purposes being a future value occurring at the beginning of the following cycle) would mean taking into account increases or decreases in value that arise after the balance sheet date. It would also mean charging replacement costs to the profit-and-loss account which, at fiscal year-end, still lie in the future. To be sure, valuing work in process at replacement cost as of turnover date would not cause any error in income calculation. Practically, the simplest solution is to accumulate historical costs in the profit-and-loss account or in a subaccount (finished goods, merchandise inventory) and to revalue them to replacement cost as of balance sheet date by charging the difference to the capital adjustment account. In that way work in process will appear in the balance sheet at year-end replacement value. If the replacement value of costs then rises or falls before turnover date, yet another correction would have to be made by debiting or crediting the capital adjustment account.